CW00551777

THROUGH STREETS BROAD AND NARROW

DR DECLAN COLLINGE

THROUGH STREETS BROAD *and* NARROW

VOICES OF DUBLIN

Declan Collinge

BEEHIVE

Published 2023 by
Beehive Books
7–8 Lower Abbey Street
Dublin 1
info@beehivebooks.ie
www.beehivebooks.ie

Beehive Books is an imprint of Veritas Publications.

Copyright © Dr Declan Collinge, 2023

ISBN 978 1 80097 048 9

10 9 8 7 6 5 4 3 2 1

The material in this publication is protected by copyright law. Except as may be permitted
by law, no part of the material may be reproduced (including by storage in a retrieval
system) or transmitted in any form or by any means, adapted, rented or lent without
the written permission of the copyright owners. Applications for permissions should be
addressed to the publisher.

A catalogue record for this book is available from the British Library.

Cover photograph of South William Street reproduced with kind permission by
artist Joby Hickey (www.jobyhickey.com); back cover photograph of the Five Lamps,
North Strand, William Murphy/Wikimedia; endpaper image is an eighteenth-century
engraving by J.J. Perret after John Rocque (c.1705–62), entitled *A Plan of the City of
Dublin and Environs in 1753*. Reproduced courtesy of the National Gallery of Ireland
(NGI.11886).

Cover design by Clare Meredith, Beehive Books
Designed and typeset by Padraig McCormack, Beehive Books
Printed in the Republic of Ireland by Walsh Colour Print, Kerry

Beehive Books is a member of Publishing Ireland.

*Beehive books are printed on paper made from the wood pulp of managed forests. For every tree
felled, at least one tree is planted, thereby renewing natural resources.*

To the memory of Danny McCarthy

'riverrun, past Eve and Adam's, from swerve of shore to bend of bay, brings us by a commodius vicus of recirculation back to Howth Castle and Environs.'

James Joyce, *Finnegans Wake*

Contents

Foreword

In the forty years since I first encountered his work, Declan Collinge has been deeply engaged, in his poetry and prose, with the identity, idioms and idiosyncrasies of his native Dublin, possessing an ability to blend his own lived experience as a Dubliner with a broad understanding of the city's past and its ever expanding future.

His committed imaginative engagement with Dublin now reaches its culmination in this new anthology, *Through Streets Broad and Narrow*. It forms a cornucopia of Dublin voices clamouring to be heard: the contemporary voices of the city and its voices that are long vanished, judiciously assembled here to explore the city's diverse past and vibrant present.

Here is blind Zozimus declaiming his words and his wares outdoors on bridges over the Liffey, a century and a half before the fashion for performance poetry emerged in the city where he died in great poverty and which has only belatedly given him a headstone. Here is Brendan Behan, by turns boisterous and brilliant, caught in the glare of his sudden fame. And Phil Lynott coming after them, a wondrous wordsmith and deeply humane force of nature, who stalked these streets like a confident, pioneering John the Baptist, paving the way for the multiracial Dublin that would gradually emerge after his death.

But here too are forgotten figures, street characters who filled out the backdrop of Dublin life for decades until one day we finally noticed they were gone. It is to Collinge's credit that his imaginative Dublin does not just exist between the canals, as tourists often see the city. A child of the new suburbs himself, he shows us their emergence in the layered comedy of Paul Howard's most famous creation, in Marie Gahan's evocative account of moving to Greenhills, in the poetry of Eileen Casey and the experiences of new arrivals from Poland, Lithuania and elsewhere.

A city like Dublin is a living, breathing and constantly changing organism, a bowl of light, a repository of hundreds of thousands of lives. Collinge's considerable achievement in this miscellany of his chosen voices is to contextualise those layers of lives, all lived one upon the other, to distil the essence of a city that is both ancient and new, forever expanding but, in this book, never losing sight of its past. There is something in this compendium to intrigue every reader. Enjoy.

Dermot Bolger
May 2023

Acknowledgements

After commending the team at Beehive Books, especially Leeann Gallagher, Padraig McCormack, Jack Carey, Kate O'Brien and Síne Quinn, as well as editor Emma Dunne and agent Michael Brennan, I should like to recognise the constant encouragement and support, over thirty years, of the late Danny McCarthy, MD of Mentor/Red Stag Books, to whom I dedicate this book, and I commend his sons, Daniel, Gerard and Kevin, for continuing his excellent work. Pádraig Ó Snodaigh of Coiscéim deserves mention for publishing most of my Irish language poetry collections. My friend the poet and historian Michael O'Flanagan and his friend Liam O'Meara, poet and historian, have never wavered in their support. I should like to thank my wife, Margaret, daughters, Nessa, Claire and Aisling, and also my own sisters and brothers for their encouragement. I am especially indebted to the immigrant writers Anna Cooper, Laura Gerulyté Griffin and Mihaela Dragan, who have provided valuable material for a new perspective on the city. My friend and fellow-musician Des Geraghty and his partner Rosheen Callender have been a constant support, as have the members of the Clé Club in Liberty Hall.

I acknowledge the support and friendship of Brendan Gibbons, whom I have known since our schooldays in Drimnagh Castle, as well as that of the late Frank Murray, whose family has been especially gracious in their endorsement. 'Renaissance man' Pat Cassidy has always been supportive, as have my former colleagues in Greenhills College. J.D. and Dympna Murphy of the Oscar Wilde Society have endorsed my work over many years, the former being an authority on the life and works of Oscar Wilde.

I am indebted to my friend Ger Andrews and his late wife, June, for their support and friendship. My college friends, Mike Cannon and Brian Finn, have given me useful advice, while a special mention must be afforded to producers Clíodhna Ní Anluain, Aoife Nic Cormaic and Sarah Binchy of *Sunday Miscellany* on RTÉ Radio, where many of my scripts were first broadcast, and to broadcasting coordinator Carolyn Dempsey and former broadcasting coordinator Geralyn Aspill, whose courtesy is much appreciated.

Dr Siegfried Bertz, who was a friend of my late father, has also provided me with interesting aspects of Dublin English. A word of thanks is due to Irish language editors Pól Ó Muirí and Éanna Ó Caolaí of the *Irish Times*, where many of my essays have been published, John Burns of the *Sunday Times* (Ireland), and Cormac Bourke and Alan English, *Sunday Independent* editors, who also published a selection of my English articles. Fellow Irish language poet Liam Prút deserves mention for writing an extensive critique of my Irish language collections, as does my former post-grad supervisor Professor Declan Kiberd, who has afforded me support and encouragement over many years.

Lastly, I acknowledge the love and affection of my ten grandchildren, who are a constant inspiration.

Custom House
Quay by Alphonse
Dousseau, c.1830–69.

Introduction

As a third-generation Dubliner who has lived in Dublin all my life, from Inchicore where I was born, to Walkinstown, Firhouse and Templeogue, and whose father came from the Liberties, I feel I can measure the pulse of the city.

My own experience of Dublin has been diverse: as a child I cut turf with my father and grandfather on the Featherbed mountain and my first summer job, at the age of thirteen, was on Dorans' farm off Tymon Lane, thinning mangolds at a shilling a drill. A visit to the mountains was as exciting as a visit to the seaside, and I recall the sense of independence which a bus journey to the city centre allowed once I was old enough to travel there with my friends. City, sea and mountains, then, were a unique feature of Dublin.

Dublin is steeped in history from its original Viking origins to the Battle of Clontarf, during which time Norsemen were assimilated into the Irish population. Its ancient walls have seen the rebellion of Silken Thomas Fitzgerald, the Irish Confederate War of 1641, the Cromwellian conquest of 1649–53, the 1798 Rebellion, Robert Emmet's uprising, the 1916 Rising, the Anglo-Irish War and the bloody Civil War.

In the world of literature, the city has boasted such writers as Jonathan Swift and Richard Brinsley

Sheridan, James Clarence Mangan and Bram Stoker, W.B. Yeats and James Joyce, Samuel Beckett, G.B. Shaw and J.M. Synge, as well as modern writers such as Brendan Behan, Austin Clarke, Maeve Binchy, Paula Meehan and Dermot Bolger, to name but a few.

James Joyce called the city 'the seventh city of Christendom'. He believed it was large enough to be a representative capital and small enough to be viewed as a whole: 'For myself, I always write about Dublin, because if I can get to the heart of Dublin I can get to the heart of all the cities of the world. In the particular is contained the universal.' His iconic novel, *Ulysses*, bears this out.

The Dublin accent echoes Elizabethan English from the time that English soldiers were billeted in the city and whose pronunciation patterns were assumed by the native Irish. This accent is now in decline as it is being threatened by the homogenised, largely American accent that is so common among young people today.

I still recall the many street rhymes which delighted my childhood play, from 'Red Rover, Red Rover, we call Paddy over', and 'Wall flowers, wall flowers, growing up so high', to the concluding mantra 'All in, all in, the game is broke up'.

While childhood in the 1950s and '60s was spartan, our wonderful Dublin communities worked almost like extended families, where a key could be left in the hall door to accommodate visitors at any time, unannounced. Such trust is now a thing of the past, but the Dubliner still retains a big heart, a spirit of generosity that is unrivalled, and an easy wit which manifests itself in razor-sharp riposte.

In selecting material for this book, where appropriate, I have included some of my own published material, from poems and radio scripts to newspaper articles. I feel honoured, therefore, to be among so many distinguished writers and poets.

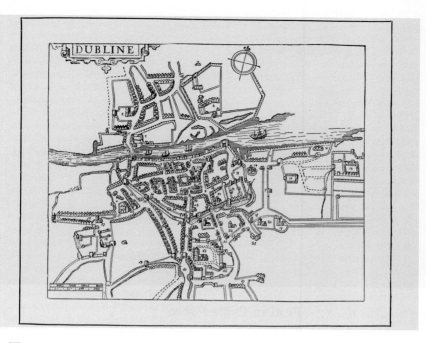

Dublin, *c.*1610.

The sequence of material used is, generally, chronological, but when an historic topic and a modern topic were related, I chose to juxtapose both.

Dublin is now a very cosmopolitan city with an immigrant population from as far afield as Asia, Central Europe and Africa, many of whom speak Irish, play Gaelic Athletic Association games and enjoy Irish dancing. While many sigh for 'Dublin in the rare ould times', the future is very promising, and we look to the generations to come to prolong the spirit of this wonderful city.

In writing this book, on such a diverse topic, I was aware that I could include only a fraction of literary material, anecdote and song which are germane to the city, but I have done my best to select what I consider to be worthy subject matter for inclusion. I have, for this reason, begun the anthology approximately in the seventeenth century. Where Dublin or Irish colloquialisms occur in the text I have added explanatory notes to ensure that all readers, inside or outside Ireland, will understand fully the excerpts included.

A Breezy Day: Howth Head by William Orpen, 1909.

Fenian Cycle Poem

This anonymous twelfth-century poem places the picturesque Hill of Howth in early Irish Fenian Cycle nature poetry. It is one of a series of poems in which St Patrick is in conversation with Oisín, son of Fionn Mac Cumhaill. Oisín has come back from the Land of Youth and is now over three hundred years old. Both old men engage in a dialogue known as Agallamh na Seanórach (Dialogue of the Elders) where Oisín praises the pre-Chistian life of his father while St Patrick advocates the Christian ethos. Dinnseanchas (topography/lore of place) is central to their conversation. These medieval poems are difficult to translate given their use of multiple adjectives, internal rhymes and assonance.

Aoibhinn Bheith i mBinn Éadair

Aoibhinn bheith i mBinn Éadair,
fírbhinn bheith ós a bhánmhuir,
cnoc lánmhar longmhar líonmhar,
beann fhíonmhar fhonnmhar ághmhar.

Beann i mbíodh Fionn is Fianna,
beann i mbíodh cuirn is cuacha,

beann i rug ua Duinn dána
lá Gráinne de rinn ruaga.

Beann tomghlas seach gach tulach
's a mullach comhghlas corrach,
cnoc lannach creamhach crannach,
beann bhallach mhíolach mhongach.

Beann is áille ós úir Éireann,
glébheann ós fharraige fhaoileann,
a tréigean is céim cráidh liom,
beann álainn Éadair aoibhinn.

Bliss to Be on Howth Head
Bliss to be on Howth Head,
   delightful
to be above its foaming sea, on the
   broad
crowded height with ships sailing
   below,
that lovely hill where wine was drunk after battle.

*St Patrick Bade his
Scribe Write All
Carefully Down* by
Stephen Reid, 1910.

The hill where Fionn and the Fianna
gathered, raising horns and goblets,
that peak where the bold Ó Duibhne
took Grainne with him in full flight.

A summit more verdant than any other,
of constant hue with many peaks, a hill
where swords and spears were brandished,
a summit of wild garlic and animals in its long
   grasses.

The fairest hill in all Ireland,
gleaming above its sweeping gulls,
to leave it is my torment,
beautiful, delightful Hill of Howth.

(*Translated by Declan Collinge*)

Grand Canal.

A Brief History of Dublin

The city appears to have grown, initially, from an ecclesiastical settlement on the River Liffey known as Duibhlinn (dark tidal pool). A subsequent Viking settlement, in the ninth century, was called Dyflin and this is believed to have been located at the confluence of the rivers Liffey and Poddle, near Dublin Castle. The later, more common Irish language name of Baile Átha Cliath (town of the ford of hurdles) probably refers to a forded crossing point near the present-day Father Mathew Bridge.

The Slighe Cualann, one of five roads which led to the high king's palace at Tara, ran through Dublin to cross the River Liffey and then turn south through the Cuala district near Bray, County Wicklow.

The city expanded in the Middle Ages from the small Viking settlement to a larger town which was well fortified. By the eleventh century, important trading routes had been established with such English towns as Chester and Bristol. After the Norman invasion of 1169 to support Leinster king Dermot Mac Murrough, the Earl of Pembroke (Strongbow) captured the city.

Its status as a city was further enhanced when King Henry II mounted a larger invasion of Ireland in 1171. A fire destroyed the city in 1190, but by the thirteenth century, Dublin was further fortified when Dublin Castle was built on the instructions of King John, in 1204. By 1220 the city had its own mayor and its prosperity increased with a population of 8,000 by the late thirteenth century.

In 1348 the Black Death ravaged Europe and also killed thousands in Dublin. The city became the centre of the Pale, a narrow strip of English settlement along the east coast. Native Irish tribes regularly attacked this area, so Dublin Castle was a major defence.

The Tudor conquest of Ireland in the sixteenth century saw Dublin rise to prominence as the administrative capital of Ireland, and the determination of Queen Elizabeth I to establish the Protestant religion in Ireland meant the founding of Trinity College in 1592, while St Patrick's and Christchurch cathedrals became Protestant churches. By 1700, a lucrative woollen and linen trade with England further strengthened the city's commerce and the population grew to over 50,000.

In Georgian times fashionable large houses and broader streets adorned the city centre. Guinness stout was brewed, and transport was improved with a stagecoach service to towns outside Dublin. By 1800 the Grand Canal and O'Connell Bridge had been built. Although the population had swollen to 200,000, poverty and disease ravaged the city.

The grandeur of the Georgian buildings diminished in the nineteenth century when the Act of Union of 1800 saw the Irish parliament move to London, leaving these buildings eventually to become tenements populated by very poor families.

After the Easter Rising of 1916, the War of Independence and the Civil War of 1921–22, the Irish Free State was established, and later the Republic of Ireland. Dublin City was at the centre of these historic events, with the GPO key to the 1916 Rising and Leinster House becoming the seat of government.

The 1930s, '40s and '50s saw economic decline, with over half a million people emigrating, but by the 1960s economic recovery halted this decline and new suburbs began to sprawl outwards from the city. This economic boom continued into the 1990s, when massive development accompanied the city's expansion and Dublin became a conurbation with 1.2 million people living in its greater area.

The economic downturn of 2009 set emigration from the city in motion once more as building in Dublin ground to a halt, but in recent years, the recovery has seen building recover, the Luas transport system expand and a more cosmopolitan city evolve with many nationalities working and living here.

Dublin City Coat of Arms

Dublin City coat of arms.

This depicts three burning castles on a shield, with a female figure standing at either side. One holds a scales (depicting justice) while the other holds a sword (representing law). The coat of arms is believed to be over four hundred years old and there has been much speculation as to what the three burning castles signify. Suggestions have been made that they commemorate the former gates of the city, with the flames recalling the defence of Dublin from the incursions of the native Irish tribes of Wicklow. Others believe that three is a lucky number, hence three castles, but a more mundane explanation could well be that, in heraldry, spaces were often filled by repetition of motifs. The Latin motto reads *Obedientia Civium Urbis Felicitas* and roughly translated means 'The obedience of the citizens makes for a happy city'. The coat of arms can be seen outside the Mansion House in Dawson Street and at the entrance to City Hall on Dame Street, among other places.

O'Connell Bridge.

CHAPTER 1

Early Dublin – Seventeenth and Eighteenth Centuries

The early seventeenth century was marked by unrest in Dublin. The English authorities prevented an attempt by the earls of Tyrone and Tyrconnell to take the city, after which both earls fled to mainland Europe. In the failed Irish rising of 1641, the rebels' plan to take Dublin Castle was foiled. In 1649 Cromwell and his forces arrived in Dublin to begin his bloody invasion of Ireland. By the end of this century Dublin was the capital of the Kingdom of Ireland with an Anglo-Irish Protestant ruling class.

Oliver Cromwell.

By contrast, the eighteenth century was a period of relative peace and prosperity in Dublin. Restrictions on industry and commerce were suspended and the rich Georgian streets and facades were constructed. When the American War of Independence commenced in 1775, large numbers of British troops were withdrawn from Ireland and the Irish parliament (in the present Bank of Ireland building on College Green) became more independent and inclusive. The rising of 1798 was planned to begin in Dublin but, due to intelligence from informants, the rebels' plans were thwarted by the government's deployment of a large military force to the city before the rebellion even began.

Richard Head

Richard Head (1637–86) was a famous writer of the seventeenth century. Born in Ireland, he is best known for his satirical novel *The English Rogue*, published in 1665. His father was killed in the Irish rising of 1641. Head moved to England when young, but was forced to flee back to Ireland because of a gambling addiction. The following is a most unflattering report by Head on his arrival in Dublin in the seventeenth century.

Dublin in the Seventeenth Century

The former parliament building, College Green.

We landed at a place called Ringsend about a mile from Dublin. I was asked whether I would have a coach. 'Where are they?' said I, for I looked about me and could see nothing like a coach. The fellow looked upon me to be a very ignorant person, because I understood not what he meant, and angrily spake thus: 'By my gossip's hand, thou canst not see very much well, arre look here is one by thy own side.' It was a great while before I could tell what language he spoke, he did so tone his words; neither could I understand him, till one standing by interpreted him. As for his Ringsend coach, as he called it, it was wheel-barrow fashion, only it had two wheels not much bigger than a large Cheshire cheese. The horse that drew this princely pygmy chariot, I at first mistook for an overgrown mastiff, but viewing him narrowly, found him the extract (by his shape) of a Scotch hobby. Well, up I mounted, but could not invent a name for the manner of my riding for I was neither coached nor carted, but I fancied myself (and that justly) as I was riding, to be some notorious malefactor drawn on a sledge to the place of execution, which afterwards experimentally I found Dublin to be. Many of its inhabitants call this city Divlin, quasi Divels Inn, and very properly it is by them so termed; for there is hardly a city in the world that entertains such variety of devil's imps as that doth. If any knavishly break, murder, rob, or are desirous of polygamy, they straightway repair thither, making that place, or the kingdom in general, their asylum, or sanctuary.

The Huguenot Cemetery, Merrion Row

After the Reformation the Protestant religion spread rapidly to France. One group of Calvinists who practised Protestantism were the Huguenots. Henry IV's Edict of Nantes (1598) granted freedom of religion to such Protestants, but after this was revoked in 1685 by Louis XIV, Huguenots were persecuted, forced to remain in France and to convert to Catholicism. Many fled France illegally to such countries as Germany, Switzerland, Holland, Great Britain and Ireland. About five thousand Huguenots came to Ireland in the late seventeenth century. Many of them settled in Dublin and Cork, as well as in other cities.

The Huguenot Cemetery in Dublin, which dates back to 1693, is located on the corner of Stephen's Green and Merrion Row. Over the years, this cemetery fell into a state of disrepair, but in 1988 the historian

The Huguenot Cemetery, Merrion Row.

Jean Paul Pitton restored it and recorded the names of the twenty-four families who had arrived in Dublin in 1681. Within a hundred years many of these original Huguenots had married into English-speaking families, but some names which did not become anglicised are still extant today, such as Lemass, Le Fanu, L'Estrange, La Touche and so on.

As well as specialising in textile manufacture and other trades, many of the Huguenot families went into finance, being instrumental in the setting up of banks in the nineteenth century. The linen trade in the north of Ireland, which made Irish linen world famous, owes its success to Huguenot labour.

George Bernard Shaw is said to have visited the cemetery in Dublin, where he noted the surname Du Bedat and then used it as the name of a couple in his famous play *The Doctor's Dilemma* – Jennifer and Louis Dubedat being the characters in question.

While the Du Bedat family motto is *Sans tache* ('Without stain'), Frank Du Bedat, a prominent stockbroker who was once president of the Dublin Stock Exchange, was jailed for bankruptcy and fraud in 1891. He died later in South Africa in 1919.

George Bernard Shaw by John Collier, 1927. *Reproduced courtesy of the National Gallery of Ireland.*

Seán Lemass, who served as taoiseach (prime minister) from 1959–66, had a notable Huguenot surname, as had the Nobel laureate playwright Samuel Beckett, whose name derives from the surname Becquett.

Eavan Boland

Eavan Boland was professor of English at Stanford University. An award-winning poet and author, her poems are often prescribed on the Leaving Cert course for Irish students. She died in 2020.

The following poem, from her collection *A Poet's Dublin* (2016), considers the sombre Huguenot Cemetery in the bustling heart of the city and the poignance of a people displaced from their native land by persecution.

The Huguenot Graveyard at the Heart of the City

It is the immodesty we bring to these
names which have eased into ours, and
their graves in the alcove of twilight,
which shadows their exile.

There is a flattery in being a destination.
There is a vanity in being the last resort.
They fled the Edict of Nantes –
hiding their shadows on the roads from France –

and now under brambles and granite
faith lies low with the lives it
dispossessed, and the hands it emptied out,
and the sombre dances they were joined in.

The buses turn right at Stephen's Green.
Car exhausts and sirens fill the air. See
the planted wildness of their rest and
grant to them the least love asks of

the living. Say: *they had another life once.*
And think of them as they first heard of us:
huddled around candles and words failing as
the stubborn tongue of the South put

oo and *an* to the sounds of Dublin,
and of their silver fingers at the window-sill
in the full moon as they leaned out
to breathe the sweet air of Nimes

for the last time, and the flame
burned down in a dawn agreed upon
for their heart-broken leave-taking. And,
for their sakes accept in that moment

this city with its colours of sky and day –
and which is dear to us and particular –
was not a place to them: merely
the one witty step ahead of hate which

is all that they could keep. Or stay.

Jonathan Swift

Jonathan Swift (1667–1745) was an Irish satirist, essayist, poet and author. He was also a cleric and dean of St Patrick's Cathedral in Dublin. He is best known for being the author of *Gulliver's Travels* (1726). In the following extract from *An Examination of Certain Abuses, Corruptions and Enormities in the City of Dublin* (1732) Swift complains about the lack of honesty among Dublin's street criers.

On Street Criers

And first there was never known a wiser institution than that of allowing certain persons of both sexes in large and populous cities to cry through the streets many necessaries of life; it would be endless to recount the conveniences which our city enjoys by this useful invention, and particularly strangers, forced hither by business, who reside here but a short time; for these having usually but little money, and being wholly ignorant of the town, might at an easy price purchase a tolerable dinner, if the several criers would pronounce the names of the goods they have to sell in any tolerable language. And therefore till our law-makers shall think it proper to interpose so far as to make these traders pronounce their words in such terms that a Christian hearer may comprehend what is cried, I would advise all newcomers to look out at their garret windows, and there see whether the thing that is cried be tripe or

flummery,[1] buttermilk or cowheels. For, as things are now managed, how is it possible for an honest countryman, just arrived, to find out what is meant for instance by the following words, with which his ears are constantly stunned twice a day, 'Mugs, jugs and porringers,[2] up in the garret and down in the cellar.' I say, how is it possible for any stranger to understand that this jargon is meant as an invitation to buy a farthing's worth of milk for his breakfast or supper, unless his curiosity draws him to the window, or till his landlady shall inform him? I produce this only as one instance, among a hundred much worse, I mean where the words make a sound wholly inarticulate, which give so much disturbance and so little information.

Hoey's Court, birthplace of Jonathan Swift.

1 A sweet dish made with beaten eggs, milk, sugar and flavourings.

2 A small bowl.

The affirmation solemnly made in the cry of herrings is directly against all truth and probability: 'Herrings alive, alive here.' The very proverb will convince us of this; for what is more frequent in ordinary speech than to say of some neighbour for whom the passing bell rings that he is 'dead as a herring.' And pray, how is it possible that a herring, which as philosophers observe cannot live longer than one minute, three seconds and a half out of water should bear a voyage in open boats from Howth to Dublin, be tossed into twenty hands and preserve its life in sieves for several hours? Nay, we have witnesses ready to produce that many thousands of these herrings, so impudently asserted to be alive, have been a day and a night upon dry land. But this is not the worst. What can we think of those impious wretches who dare in the face of the sun vouch the very same affirmative of their salmon and cry 'Salmon, alive, alive'; whereas if you call the woman who cries it she is not ashamed to turn back her mantle and show you this individual salmon cut into a dozen pieces. I have given good advice to these infamous disgracers of their sex and calling without the least appearance of remorse, and fully against the conviction of their own consciences. I have mentioned the grievance to several of our parish ministers, but all in vain; so that it must continue till the Government shall think fit to interpose.

St Patrick's Cathedral, Wood Quay

Built on the site of a holy well associated with St Patrick, this famous church attained cathedral status in 1203. It was further renovated between 1220 and 1260 but, over the centuries, suffered neglect and constant dampness. During the sixteenth century some of the cathedral's contents were destroyed on the order of Henry VIII, and Cromwell himself was reputed to have used the building as a stable for his soldiers' horses. The spire of the cathedral was added in 1749, after which Sir Benjamin Lee Guinness undertook a much more extensive restoration between 1860 and 1865.

In 1492 a dispute arose between the Butler family of Ormond (from the Kilkenny–Tipperary area) and the Fitzgerald family of Kildare, since both families wanted one of their own to hold the position of lord deputy. The situation escalated and a small skirmish occurred outside the walls of Dublin.

As the battle raged the Butlers took refuge in the Chapter House of St Patrick's Cathedral. The Fitzgeralds demanded that they come out and make peace but the Butlers refused, fearing slaughter.

Gerard Fitzgerald, head of the Kildare family, then had a hole cut in the door of the Chapter House. He thrust his arm through the door and offered to shake hands as a gesture of goodwill. Both families then shook hands through the door and made peace.

Monuments to Jonathan Swift and Stella, St Patrick's Cathedral, 1840.

The door is on display today in the north transept of the cathedral and it is known as 'the door of reconciliation'. The expression to 'chance your arm', meaning to undertake something even when the outcome may be dangerous or unsuccessful, is said to derive from this incident in 1492.

The cathedral is now most famous for the fact that Jonathan Swift was dean here from 1713 to 1745. Swift's grave and that of his partner Stella (Esther Johnson) can be seen in the south aisle, just inside the door of the cathedral. Polished brass plaques mark these graves. The following is Swift's epitaph, which appears nearby in Latin:

Hic depositum est Corpus
Ionathan Swift S.T.D.
Hujus Ecclesiæ Cathedralis

Decani
Ubi sæva Indignatio
Ulterius
Cor lacerare nequit.
Abi Viator
Et imitare, si poteris,
Strenuum pro virili
Libertatis Vindicatorem.

This translates as:

Here lies the body of Jonathan Swift, Doctor of
Sacred Theology, dean of this cathedral church where
savage rage can no longer tear his heart. Go traveller
and imitate if you can a brave champion of manly
freedom.

W.B. Yeats's translation is more poetic:

SWIFT has sailed into his rest;
Savage indignation there
Cannot lacerate his breast.
Imitate him if you dare,
World-besotted traveller; he
Served human liberty.

In his will Swift decreed that his money should
provide for a psychiatric hospital. The original hospital
has since become St Patrick's Mental Health Services
and includes a variety of locations. The following witty
lines by Swift describe this bequest:

He gave the little wealth he had
to build a House for Fools and Mad
and show'd by one satiric touch
no Nation wanted it so much.
That kingdom he hath left his debtor,
I wish it soon may have a better.

In 2018 HRSI (Human Remains Services Ireland) recreated the faces of Jonathan Swift and Stella by using Swift's death mask and the skull cast of Stella.

Fishlass

The following Dublin street song tells the story of a young street crier who sold fish in the city. Some have speculated that her 'dying of a fever' implies that she was a sex worker who died of syphilis. In 1988, to mark the millennium of Dublin City, Jeanne Rynhart (1946–2020) designed the bronze statue which now stands outside the Dublin tourist office on Suffolk Street. It depicts a voluptuous woman, dressed in seventeenth-century clothing, pushing her cart of fish. The statue is known colloquially as 'The Trollop with the Scallop' or 'The Tart with the Cart'. The song 'Molly Malone' is regularly sung as a sporting anthem by the supporters of the Dublin GAA team and by those of Bohemian FC as well as Ireland rugby supporters.

Molly Malone

In Dublin's fair city
where the girls are so pretty
I first set my eyes on sweet Molly Malone
as she wheeled her wheelbarrow
through streets broad and narrow
crying 'Cockles and mussels, alive, alive, oh.'

Alive, alive, oh
alive, alive, oh
crying 'Cockles and mussels, alive, alive, oh.'

She was a fishmonger
and sure, 'twas no wonder
for so were her mother and father before
and they both wheeled their barrows
through streets broad and narrow
crying 'Cockles and mussels, alive, alive, oh.'

Molly Malone by
Jeanne Rynhart.

Alive, alive, oh
alive, alive, oh
crying 'Cockles and mussels, alive, alive, oh.'

But she died of a fever
and no one could save her
and that was the end of sweet Molly Malone.
Now her ghost wheels the barrow
through streets broad and narrow
crying 'Cockles and mussels, alive, alive oh.'

Alive, alive, oh
alive, alive, oh
crying 'Cockles and mussels, alive, alive, oh.'

The *Ouzel Galley*

On an autumn morning in 1695 the merchant ship
Ouzel Galley sailed out of Ringsend, Dublin, on a
trading mission, bound for the port of Smyrna (now
Izmir in Turkey) on the Anatolian coast. Its captain
was Eoghan Massey of Waterford.

Three years later, when the vessel still had not returned to Dublin, it was presumed to have been lost at sea and a settlement was made between the owner of the ship and the underwriters. The three officers and crew of thirty-seven were all declared dead and insurance money was paid in full.

In 1700, however, Dubliners were amazed to see the *Ouzel Galley* sail up the River Liffey and land at Ringsend once more. Captain Massey and his crew told how their vessel had been commandeered by Algerian pirates. They claimed they were taken prisoner and forced to work with the pirates as they plundered other ships.

The *Ouzel Galley* and the pirate ship.

While the pirates went ashore to carouse, however, the captive crew of the *Ouzel Galley* overpowered their guards and hoisted the sails to escape and head for home. The hold of the galley was full of pirate spoils, increasing the value of the ship considerably.

Since the vessel was now worth more than its original value, and since it was illegal to divide plunder among the crew, the arbitration body which had settled the insurance claim two years earlier reconvened and decided that a society should be formed to fund relief for needy merchants. Entitled 'The Ouzel Galley Society', it mediated industrial disputes and contributed to the construction of Dublin City Hall in 1761 (then known as the Royal Exchange). By 1783 the Dublin Chamber of Commerce had been established and this was in no small part due to the influence of the Ouzel Galley Society. In time the society became defunct, and its final funds were divided among the city hospitals.

Over the years many considered the story of the *Ouzel Galley* too far-fetched to be true: the capture of the galley by pirates, the five years' forced labour and the dramatic escape all seemed more fiction than fact. One explanation of the *Ouzel Galley* story was that Captain Massey had falsely named the port of Smyrna as their destination when he really intended to trade in the Caribbean. This was a very dangerous area in which to trade, with piracy rampant. It is possible that Massey and his crew had themselves plundered other ships and used the story of their capture by Algerian pirates to explain the booty in the hold on their return to Dublin.

If so, then the plan may have backfired: many of the ship's crew returned to find that their wives, presuming they were dead, had remarried and had had children by their new spouses – in fact, such children were known as 'Ouzelers', a term used for years afterwards in Ringsend for children born in unusual circumstances.

A sculpted ship can still be seen on a building in Dame Street, representing the galley and its colourful voyage. This reminds visitors of the strange story of the galley and the consequences for its crew.

CHAPTER 2

The Gothic Masters

Gothic literature usually involves themes of horror, death and decay, as well as ghosts, vampires and other supernatural elements. Madness and violence, family curses and settings in old, decrepit houses and castles are all common features of the genre. Dublin has produced a number of masterpieces of Gothic literature, such as Joseph Sheridan Le Fanu's *Carmilla*, Charles Maturin's *Melmoth the Wanderer*, Oscar Wilde's *The Picture of Dorian Gray* and, of course, the most famous: Bram Stoker's *Dracula*, which has inspired countless vampire stories and horror films over the years.

Lippincott's Monthly Magazine, July 1890, featuring the first publication of *The Picture of Dorian Gray* by Oscar Wilde; *Dracula* by Bram Stoker, 1897.

The Hellfire Club

On the top of Montpelier Hill, in the Dublin Mountains, sits an old ruin. This is the remains of a hunting lodge built in 1725 by the Right Honourable Sir William Conolly (1662–1729), speaker in the Irish House of Commons. Conolly, reputedly one of the richest men in Ireland at the time, erected the hunting lodge using stones from an ancient cairn and passage grave which lay nearby. Shortly after its construction,

Ruins of the hunting lodge used by the Hellfire Club, 2010.

during a storm, the wooden roof was blown off the building. Local people claimed that this was the vengeance of whatever spirits inhabited the cairn, but Conolly ignored their superstitious concerns and replaced the original with a strong stone roof which was guaranteed to stand the test of time.

After Conolly's death in 1729, his widow, Katherine, leased the hunting lodge to Richard Parsons, 1st Earl of Rosse. Parsons, known for his hedonistic lifestyle, founded a branch of the Hellfire Club in Dublin. These clubs had been first set up in England in 1718, and their aristocratic members involved themselves in such activities as mock religious ceremonies, heavy drinking and debauchery.

Some members of the Irish Hellfire Club used the hunting lodge on Montpelier Hill for their hedonistic excesses. It was reported that Parsons regularly attended dressed in devil's garb with horns and wings and that an empty place was always left for Satan at the table. Some of the more extreme events involved drenching a cat in alcohol and setting it alight, as well as doing the same to a servant. The former may well explain the story of an enormous black cat associated with the building. Then there was the frequently told story of Satan's appearance at the club: some men were playing cards there when a dark stranger entered and asked to play. As the card game continued, one man dropped the ace of spades and bent down to retrieve it. While under the table, he noticed that the stranger had a cloven hoof for a foot. He jumped up and screamed, making for the door. The stranger then disappeared in a puff of smoke. Since that time the hunting lodge itself has been called 'the Hellfire Club'.

There has been speculation that these stories were deliberately fabricated and spread to scare away local people from the building, especially during the heyday of body-snatching in the late eighteenth century. As the exhumed bodies would be sold to doctors for medical science, the grave robbers reputedly used the hunting lodge to store the corpses until a sale could be made. The satanic reputation of the lodge guaranteed that the robbers remained undisturbed.

In more recent times archaeologists from Abarta Heritage have excavated the ground around the Hellfire Club and discovered a 5,000-year-old passage tomb. It is believed that a number of these tombs had been constructed on other summits also in the Dublin Mountains.

In 2017 there were protests against the plan by South Dublin County Council and Coillte to build a €19 million tourist centre on the site of the Hellfire Club. Local people claimed that run-off from the centre might cause flooding in the surrounding area, while others simply wanted the building left as it had been for almost three hundred years.

The following poem from my collection *Fearful Symmetry* fondly recalls a night in the mid-sixties when Frank Murray and I were so engrossed in conversation that we walked further and further out beyond Walkinstown, Dublin, until we had reached Tallaght Village – then a rural village. Frank and I were friends since childhood. Years later he became manager of the Pogues. The lines are particularly poignant now, since Frank passed away suddenly in December 2016.

To Tallaght and the Hellfire Club

A walk to Tallaght
by night
seals bonds of youthful
camaraderie;
we hike along
the Greenhills Road
braving the chill breeze,
its jagged glass
slashing our faces
watching far away
Dublin's jewelled beauty
curve into the bay.

Past the village
and the Priory cloisters
we walk in the footsteps
of Fenian dead[1]
with riotous snowflakes
smarting in our eyes.
The plague of history
is easily avoided
and relegated to the classroom;
we talk of spring and summer
of thinning mangels
on Doran's farm
or canning plums in Lambs
of sea breezes and seaside girls
striding like Andress
out of the surf.[2]

On Old Bawn bridge
we hear the swollen Dodder
coursing through the night,
ranging through time,
our only constant
in a world too fast
for pause –

1 During the Fenian (Irish Republican Brotherhood – IRB) uprising of 1867 there were skirmishes at Tallaght Village between the local police and a large group of IRB men.

2 In *Dr No*, the first James Bond film, the actor Ursula Andress appears, in an iconic scene, walking out of the waves.

By midnight we will reach the Hellfire Club
there to test our nerve
facing down the spirit of the cairn
and the one
who turned the Ace of Spades,
our broken-voiced bellows
ringing in the ruins
while the moon defines
Corrig and Seahawn
and the city twinkles
to beguile us
in distant serenity.

Le Fanu

Joseph Sheridan Le Fanu (1814–73), a Dublin writer, was famous for his gothic stories, mystery novels and horror fiction. He is the author of *Carmilla*.

The following extract from his gothic novel *The House by the Churchyard* (1863) is set in the Dublin village of Chapelizod. The local doctor's daughter, Lilias Walsingham, is going to bed. Her old servant, Sally, tells her about the haunting of the Tiled House in Ballyfermot, where the main protagonist of the novel, Mr Mervyn, is staying.

Illustration for *Carmilla* by Michael Fitzgerald.

From *The House by the Churchyard*

Old Sally always attended her young mistress while she prepared for bed – not that Lilias required help, for she had the spirit of neatness and a joyous, gentle alacrity, and only troubled the good old creature enough to prevent her thinking herself grown old and useless.

Sally, in her quiet way, was garrulous, and she had all sorts of old-world tales of wonder and adventure, to which Lilias often went pleasantly to sleep; for there was no danger while old Sally sat knitting there by the fire, and the sound of the rector's mounting upon his chairs, as was his wont, and taking down and putting up his books in the study beneath, though muffled and faint, gave evidence that that good and loving influence was awake and busy.

Old Sally was telling her young mistress, who sometimes listened with a smile, and sometimes lost a good five minutes together of her gentle prattle, how the young gentleman, Mr Mervyn, had taken that awful old, haunted habitation, the Tiled House 'beyant[3] at Ballyfermot,' and was going to stay there, and wondered no one had told him of the mysterious dangers of that desolate mansion. ...

'There are people, Sally, nowadays, who call themselves free-thinkers, and don't believe in anything – even in ghosts,' said Lilias.

'A then the place he's stopping in now, Miss Lily, 'ill soon cure him of free-thinking, if the half they say about it's true,' answered Sally.

'But I don't say, mind, he's a free-thinker, for I don't know anything of Mr. Mervyn; but if he be not, he must be very brave, or very good, indeed. I know, Sally, I should be horribly afraid, indeed, to sleep in it myself,' answered Lilias, with a cosy little shudder, as the aerial image of the old house for a moment stood before her, with its peculiar malign, sacred, and skulking aspect, as if it had drawn back in shame and guilt under the melancholy old elms among the tall hemlock and nettles.

'And now, Sally, I'm safe in bed. Stir the fire, my old darling.' For although it was the first week in May, the night was frosty. 'And tell me all about the Tiled House again and frighten me out of my wits.' ...

So she told her how when the neighbours hired the orchard that ran up to the windows at the back of the house, the dogs they kept there used to howl so wildly and wolfishly all night among the trees, and prowl under the walls of the house so dejectedly, that they were fain to open the door and let them in at last; and, indeed, small

3   Beyond.

need was there for dogs; for no one, young or old, dared go near the orchard after night-fall. No, the burnished golden pippins that peeped through the leaves in the western rays of evening and made the mouths of the Ballyfermot school-boys water, glowed undisturbed in the morning sunbeams, and secure in the mysterious tutelage of the night smiled coyly on their predatory longings. And this was no fanciful reserve and avoidance. Mick Daly, when he had the orchard, used to sleep in the loft over the kitchen; and he swore that within five or six weeks, while he lodged there, he twice saw the same thing, and that was a lady in a hood and a loose dress, her head drooping, and her finger on her lip, walking in silence among the crooked

Childhood home of Sheridan Le Fanu, Chapelizod, the inspiration for *The House by the Churchyard*.

stems, with a little child by the hand, who ran smiling and skipping beside her. And the Widow Cresswell once met them at night-fall, on the path through the orchard to the back-door, and she did not know what it was until she saw the men looking at one another as she told it.

'It's often she told it to me,' said old Sally; 'and how she came on them all of a sudden at the turn of the path, just by the thick clump of alder trees; and how she stopped, thinking it was some lady that had a right to be there; and how they went by as swift as the shadow of a cloud, though she only seemed to be walking slow enough, and the little child pulling by her arm, this way and that way, and took no notice of her, nor even raised her head, though she stopped and curtsied. And old Dalton, don't you remember old Dalton, Miss Lily?'

'I think I do, the old man who limped, and wore the old black wig?'

'Yes, indeed, acushla,[4] so he did. See how well she remembers! That was by a kick of one of the earl's horses – he was groom there,' resumed Sally. 'He used to

4 From the Irish *a chuisle* (pulse of my heart), meaning 'my darling'.

be troubled with hearing the very sounds his master used to make to bring him and old Oliver to the door, when he came back late. It was only on very dark nights when there was no moon. They used to hear all on a sudden, the whimpering and scraping of dogs at the hall door, and the sound of the whistle, and the light stroke across the window with the lash of the whip, just like as if the earl himself – may his poor soul find rest – was there. First the wind'id stop, like you'd be holding your breath, then came these sounds they knew so well, and when they made no sign of stirring or opening the door, the wind 'id begin again with such a hoo-hoo-o-o-high, you'd think it was laughing, and crying, and hooting all at once.' ...

'The very night he met his death in England, old Oliver, the butler, was listening to Dalton – for Dalton was a scholar – reading the letter that came to him through the post that day, telling him to get things ready, for his troubles wor[5] nearly over and he expected to be with them again in a few days, and maybe almost as soon as the letter; and sure enough, while he was reading, there comes a frightful rattle at the window, like someone all in a tremble, trying to shake it open, and the earl's voice, as they both conceited, cries from outside, "Let me in, let me in, let me in!" "It's him," says the butler. "Tis so, bedad," says Dalton, and they both looked at the windy,[6] and at one another – and then back again – overjoyed, in a soart of a way, and frightened all at onst. Old Oliver was bad with the rheumatiz. So away goes Dalton to the hall-door, and he calls "who's there?" and no answer. "Maybe," says Dalton, to himself, "tis what he's rid round to the back-door"; so to the back-door with him, and there he shouts again – and no answer, and not a sound outside – and he began to feel quare,[7] and to the hall door with him back again. "Who's there? do you hear? who's there?" he shouts, and receives no answer still. "I'll open the door at any rate," says he, "maybe it's what he's made his escape," for they knew all about his troubles, and wants to get in without noise, so praying all the time – for his mind misgave him it might not be all right – he shifts the

5 Were.

6 Window.

7 Queer, meaning strange.

bars and unlocks the door; but neither man, woman, nor child, nor horse, nor any living shape was standing there, only something or another slipt into the house close by his leg; it might be a dog, or something that way, he could not tell, for he only seen it for a moment with the corner of his eye, and it went in just like as if it belonged to the place. He could not see which way it went, up or down, but the house was never a happy one, or a quiet house after; and Dalton bangs the hall-door, and he took a sort of a turn and a trembling, and back with him to Oliver, the butler, looking as white as the blank leaf of his master's letter, that was between his finger and thumb. "What is it? *what* is it?" says the butler, catching his crutch like a waypon,[8] fastening his eyes on Dalton's white face, and growing almost as pale himself. "The master's dead," says Dalton – and so he was, signs on it.

'After the turn she got by what she seen in the orchard, when she came to know the truth of what it was, Jinny Cresswell, you may be sure, did not stay there an hour longer than she could help: and she began to take notice of things she did not mind before – such as when she went into the big bed-room over the hall, that the lord used to sleep in, whenever she went in at one door the other door used to be pulled to very quick, as if someone avoiding her was getting out in haste; but the thing that frightened her most was just this – that sometimes she used to find a long straight mark from the head to the foot of her bed, as if 'twas made by something heavy lying there, and the place where it was used to feel warm – as if – whoever it was – they only left it as she came into the room.

'But the worst of all was poor Kitty Haplin, the young woman that died of what she seen. Her mother said it was how she was kept awake all the night with the walking about of some one in the next room, tumbling about boxes, and pulling over drawers, and talking and sighing to himself, and she, poor thing, wishing to go asleep, and wondering who it could be, when in he comes, a fine man, in a sort of loose silk morning-dress, an' no wig, but

8 Weapon.

9 Easy.

a velvet cap on, and to the windy with him quiet and aisy,[9] and she makes a turn in the bed to let him know there was some one there, thinking he'd go away, but instead of that, over he comes to the side of the bed, looking very bad, and says something to her – but his speech was thick and choakin' like a dummy's that id be trying to spake – and she grew very frightened, and says she, "I ask your honour's pardon, Sir, but I can't hear you right," and with that he stretches up his neck nigh out of his cravat, turning his face up towards the ceiling, and – grace between us and harm! – his throat was cut across, and wide open; she seen no more, but dropped in a dead faint in the bed, and back to her mother with her in the morning, and she

10 Swallowed.

never swallied[10] bit or sup more, only she just sat by the fire holding her mother's hand, crying and trembling, and peepin' over her shoulder, and starting with every sound, till she took the fever and died, poor thing, not five weeks after.' And so on, and on, and on flowed the stream of old Sally's narrative, while Lilias dropped into dreamless sleep, and then the story-teller stole away to her own tidy bed-room and innocent slumbers.

Marsh's Library.

The Haunting of Marsh's Library

Narcissus Marsh (1638–1713), former provost of Trinity College Dublin, became archbishop of Dublin in 1694 and that of Armagh in 1703. In 1707 he founded Marsh's Library in St Patrick's Close, adjacent to St Patrick's Cathedral. Having found that many of the young scholars at Trinity were 'rude and ignorant' due to their lack of education, and that the library in the college was inadequate, he decided to build his own library which would allow free access to all interested parties. The library, with its collection of over

25,000 volumes on medicine, ancient history, theology and literature, has been used by many scholars over the years, including Jonathan Swift, Bram Stoker (writing drafts of *Dracula*) and James Joyce.

The archbishop reared his favourite niece, Grace, from childhood and she later became his housekeeper. At the age of nineteen, however, Grace Marsh fell in love with a handsome young minister and eloped with him. Prior to that she left a note for her dear uncle, begging his forgiveness, in one of the books in the library. However, despite frequent and desperate searching, the archbishop was unable to find her note. To this day, the north section of the library is considered unusually cold, and it is reported that the ghost of Archbishop Marsh has been seen in this area, apparently searching the bookshelves constantly for the note his niece left him. The library is open to the public.

Bram Stoker

In the following excerpt from *Dracula* (1897), the famous epistolary gothic novel by Clontarf-born Bram Stoker (1847–1912), Jonathan Harker, a young English lawyer who has travelled to visit Count Dracula in his castle to assist him with a legal matter, finally meets the count.

From *Dracula*

Bram Stoker, *c.*1906.

He bowed in a courtly way as he replied, 'I am Dracula, and I bid you welcome, Mr. Harker, to my house. Come in, the night air is chill, and you must need to eat and rest.' As he was speaking, he put the lamp on a bracket on the wall, and stepping out, took my luggage. He had carried it in before I could forestall him. I protested, but he insisted.

'Nay, sir, you are my guest. It is late, and my people are not available. Let me see to your comfort myself.' He insisted on carrying my traps along the passage, and then up a great winding stair, and along another great passage, on whose stone floor our steps rang heavily. At the end of this he threw open a heavy door, and I rejoiced to see within a well-lit room in which a table was spread for supper, and on whose mighty hearth a great fire of logs, freshly replenished, flamed and flared. ...

'You will need, after your journey, to refresh yourself by making your toilet. I trust you will find all you wish. When you are ready, come into the other room, where you will find your supper prepared.'

The light and warmth and the Count's courteous welcome seemed to have dissipated all my doubts and fears. Having then reached my normal state, I discovered that I was half famished with hunger. So making a hasty toilet, I went into the other room.

I found supper already laid out. My host, who stood on one side of the great fireplace, leaning against the stonework, made a graceful wave of his hand to the table, and said,

'I pray you, be seated and sup how you please. You will I trust, excuse me that I do not join you, but I have dined already, and I do not sup.'

I handed to him the sealed letter which Mr. Hawkins had entrusted to me. He opened it and read it gravely. Then, with a charming smile, he handed it to me to read. One passage of it, at least, gave me a thrill of pleasure.

'I must regret that an attack of gout, from which malady I am a constant sufferer, forbids absolutely any travelling on my part for some time to come. But I am happy to say I can send a sufficient substitute, one in whom I have every possible confidence. He is a young man, full of energy and talent in his own way, and of a very faithful disposition. He is discreet and silent, and has grown into manhood in my service. He shall be ready to attend on you when you will during his stay, and shall take your instructions in all matters.'

The count himself came forward and took off the cover of a dish, and I fell to at once on an excellent roast

chicken. This, with some cheese and a salad and a bottle of old tokay,[11] of which I had two glasses, was my supper. During the time I was eating it the Count asked me many questions as to my journey, and I told him by degrees all I had experienced.

By this time I had finished my supper, and by my host's desire had drawn up a chair by the fire and begun to smoke a cigar which he offered me, at the same time excusing himself that he did not smoke. I had now an opportunity of observing him, and found him of a very marked physiognomy. ...

Hitherto I had noticed the backs of his hands as they lay on his knees in the firelight, and they had seemed rather white and fine. But seeing them now close to me, I could not but notice that they were rather coarse, broad, with squat fingers. Strange to say, there were hairs in the centre of the palm. The nails were long and fine, and cut

The ruins of Whitby Abbey in Yorkshire, England, were an inspiration for Stoker's *Dracula*.

11 A Hungarian dessert wine.

to a sharp point. As the Count leaned over me and his hands touched me, I could not repress a shudder. It may have been that his breath was rank, but a horrible feeling of nausea came over me, which, do what I would, I could not conceal.

The Count, evidently noticing it, drew back. And with a grim sort of smile, which showed more than he had yet done his protuberant teeth, sat himself down again on his own side of the fireplace. We were both silent for a while, and as I looked towards the window I saw the first dim streak of the coming dawn. There seemed a strange stillness over everything. But as I listened, I heard as if from down below in the valley the howling of many wolves. The Count's eyes gleamed, and he said:

'Listen to them, the children of the night. What music they make!' Seeing, I suppose, some expression in my face strange to him, he added:

'Ah, sir, you dwellers in the city cannot enter into the feelings of the hunter.' Then he rose and said:

'But you must be tired. Your bedroom is all ready, and tomorrow you shall sleep as late as you will. I have to be away till the afternoon, so sleep well and dream well!' With a courteous bow, he opened for me himself the door to the octagonal room, and I entered my bedroom.

I am all in a sea of wonders. I doubt. I fear. I think strange things, which I dare not confess to my own soul. God keep me, if only for the sake of those dear to me!

Nocturnes of the Flesh

This poem is from my collection *Fearful Symmetry* (1990). It recalls how, as teenagers, we regularly went to the Apollo cinema in Walkinstown to see the Hammer Horror series. We hoped that our girlfriends would cling tightly to us during the films and that there might be some opportunity for romance later among the trees on Field Avenue – named after the famous Irish pianist and composer John Field (1782–1837) who popularised the nocturne.

Hammer Horror

The wind that howls around Castle Dracula
howls to our advantage: we huddle
in the cinema balcony, eagerly protecting
girlfriends from the scourge of the vampire
and the burning eyes of Christopher Lee.

Our master is surely renowned
for his hospitality –
his bloodshot eyes and sabre fangs
drive our sweethearts closer,
craning our necks in the perfumed dark,
to shield our trembling charges,
we gladly miss the cold debauchery
of the monster's kiss.

As he squirms and shrinks to dust
Before the Cross we mop
The sweat from our brows,
Infinitely more exhausted than
His relentless pursuer, blinking
In the theatre light
Walking our girls into the winter night.

The full moon offers endless possibilities
for gothic interlude –
wolf whistles pierce the frosted streets
where children of the night play[12]
nocturnes of the flesh
behind the trees on Field Avenue
and teenage Hammermen,
the vampire's retinue, leave marks
of the beast to shocked discerning eyes
after sunrise.

12 'Listen to them, the children of the night. What music they make.' (From *Dracula* by Bram Stoker.)

CHAPTER 3

Romantics and Rebellion – The Nineteenth Century

The dawn of the nineteenth century saw the Act of Union (1801) which merged the Irish parliament with the British parliament in London. Dublin lost its political status as a capital. From this time on the large Georgian houses in Dublin, previously owned by the ruling class, gradually fell into disrepair due to neglect. By the end of the century these buildings had become tenements housing thousands of poor Catholic families in appalling conditions. Dublin was the scene of Robert Emmet's unsuccessful Irish rebellion in 1803. The nineteenth century also saw Catholic emancipation in 1829 as well as the terrible Great Famine, 1845–1849, and the bid for Home Rule to re-establish an Irish parliament.

Flag used by Robert Emmet during the 1803 Irish rebellion.

Robert Emmet and the Irish Rebellion of 1803

Robert Emmet (1778–1803) was born into an affluent Protestant ascendancy family with a fine house on St Stephen's Green and another in Milltown. Following in the footsteps of his brother Thomas Addis Emmet, Robert joined the United Irishmen and was expelled

*July 23, 1803, Robert
Emmet Heads His
Men*, printed in *The
Shamrock*, 5 July 1890.

from Trinity College Dublin for his association with this revolutionary movement.

After the failure of the 1798 rebellion, Emmet fled to France to avoid arrest. There he tried to gain the support of Napoleon in the Irish struggle against British rule. While Napoleon initially promised support, he did not deliver, as he was concentrating on invading England.

Emmet hoped to instigate a further rebellion in the year 1803. He had hoped that fellow United Irishman Michael O'Dwyer and his men in Wicklow would march on Dublin and augment his followers. The plans for the rising were kept secret but some unstable material at a premises in Patrick Street exploded prematurely, leading the authorities to investigate.

In late July 1803, Emmet and his men tried, unsuccessfully, to take Dublin Castle. However, due to a communications failure, O'Dwyer and his rebels did not come to support Emmet. Other rebels in Kildare turned back because they were uncertain of the supply of weapons. The rising deteriorated into a skirmish in Thomas Street, during which the Lord Chief Justice of Ireland, Thomas Kilwarden, was dragged from his carriage and stabbed. The rising soon fell apart and Emmet fled. While visiting his fiancée Sarah Curran in Harold's Cross, Emmet was captured and tried for high treason by Lord Norbury, who was known as 'the hanging judge'.

During his trial Emmet made a powerful speech from the dock which has since become iconic among republicans:

Let ... my tomb remain uninscribed, and my memory in oblivion, until other times and other men can do justice to my character. When my country takes her place among the nations of the earth, then and not till then, let my epitaph be written. I have done.

Trial of Robert Emmet, Emmet Replying to the Verdict of High Treason, Sept. 19 1803, nineteenth-century engraving.

After he was hanged outside St Catherine's Church in Thomas Street, Emmet was beheaded. Shortly after this his body went missing. It was believed at the time that Emmet's remains were buried in St Michan's churchyard in Church Street, but no one to this day knows precisely where his final resting place is.

Shelley on Emmet

In 1812 the Romantic poet Percy Bysshe Shelley travelled to Ireland with his wife Harriet and stayed in rooms in O'Connell Street (then Sackvillle Street) and in Grafton Street. Here he distributed 1,500 copies of a pamphlet entitled 'An Address to the Irish People'. In this, Shelley outlined his own revolutionary views and hoped that the Irish might continue to fight for Irish freedom.

Unfortunately, by then most of the United Irishmen had been arrested and those that remained at large had no appetite for further fighting. Shelley did speak at a public meeting of the Catholic Association in Fishamble Street, sharing a platform with 'The Liberator', Daniel O'Connell.

As Shelley admired Emmet's revolutionary zeal and was saddened by his brutal execution, he visited St Michan's churchyard, where he believed Emmet was buried. He was inspired to compose the following poem.

On Robert Emmet's Grave
No trump tells thy virtues – the grave where they rest
With thy dust shall remain unpolluted by fame,
Till thy foes, by the world and by fortune caressed,
Shall pass like a mist from the light of thy name.

When the storm-cloud that lowers o'er the day-beam
    is gone,
Unchanged, unextinguished its life-spring will shine;
When Erin has ceased with their memory to groan,
She will smile through the tears of revival on thine.

James Clarence
Mangan bust, St
Stephen's Green.

James Clarence Mangan

James Clarence Mangan (1803–49) was born the son of a grocer in upper Fishamble Street. Tutored initially by a Jesuit father, Mangan learned the basics of Latin, French, Spanish and Italian. After his father became bankrupt Mangan went to work as a scrivener for a solicitor in York Street. In time he began writing and submitted scripts to literary magazines. He distinguished himself as a translator and his finest work was his translation of the Irish language poem 'Róisín Dubh', which he translated as 'My Dark Rosaleen'. Mangan used laudanum and drank heavily. He fell victim to a cholera epidemic in 1849 and, given his poor health, died at the age of forty-three.

The poem/song 'Róisín Dubh' dates back to the sixteenth century. The early version of the poem was simply a love poem to the poet's beloved, but the song eventually acquired political significance, serving as a metaphor for Ireland, where the hope of delivery from British oppression by Spain or France was expressed. The song is often sung a cappella as a sean-nós melody. Seán Ó Riada scored an orchestral version of the melody for *Mise Éire* (a film about Irish history) in 1959.

My Dark Rosaleen

O my dark Rosaleen,
Do not sigh, do not weep!
The priests are on the ocean green,
They march along the deep.
There's wine from the royal Pope,
Upon the ocean green;
And Spanish ale shall give you hope,
My Dark Rosaleen!
My own Rosaleen!

Shall glad your heart, shall give you hope,
Shall give you health, and help, and hope,
My Dark Rosaleen! ...

O, the Erne shall run red,
With redundance of blood,
The earth shall rock beneath our tread,
And flames wrap hill and wood,

And gun-peal and slogan-cry
Wake many a glen serene,
Ere you shall fade, ere you shall die,
My Dark Rosaleen!

My own Rosaleen!
The Judgement Hour must first be nigh,
Ere you can fade, ere you can die,
My Dark Rosaleen!

The Pride and Prejudice of Thomas Langlois Lefroy

Illustration for
Pride and Prejudice,
engraving after
Ferdinand Pickering.

Thomas Langlois Lefroy (1776–1869) was born in Limerick to a Huguenot family. He attended Trinity College Dublin and distinguished himself as an outstanding student. He studied law at Lincoln's Inn in London and later held many prestigious positions in Ireland, such as auditor of the History Society in Trinity College and, later, Lord Chief Justice in 1852. As he was seventy-six years of age at that time, many argued that Lefroy was too old for the position, but he disregarded these reservations and held the post doggedly until he was ninety – a mere three years before his death. He opposed the Catholic Relief Act of 1829 and presided over the trial for sedition of the Young Ireland leader John Mitchel.

When Lefroy was a young man, in 1796, he holidayed in Hampshire and was a frequent visitor to the parsonage at Steventon where he was introduced to Jane Austen, who was two years older than he. The young couple related very well to each other, singing duets and dancing together. Given that this was around the time that Jane Austen wrote her famous novel *Pride and Prejudice*, many believe that Fitzwilliam Darcy in that novel was based on the character of Thomas Langlois Lefroy, while that of Elizabeth Bennet was based on Jane Austen herself.

Austen mentions Lefroy in some of her letters and admits that she cried when he returned to Ireland without mentioning marriage. Such a marriage would never have met with the approval of the Lefroy family, since Jane's dowry would have been very meagre.

If Mr Darcy is proud and haughty then perhaps Jane Austen modelled him correctly, since the older Lord Chief Justice was opinionated and quite prejudiced. In fact, his exit from the bench in Ireland was dignified only because he placed his resignation in the hands of the new prime minister, Lord Stanley, who promptly accepted it without reservation.

Lefroy's nephew wrote about his uncle's relationship with Jane Austen. According to him Thomas Langlois Lefroy was 'in love with Jane Austen', but it was 'a boyish love'. When Jane Austen died in 1817 Lefroy did travel to England to pay his respects. He would die himself at the age of ninety-three, fifty-two years later.

The Night of the Big Wind

Perhaps the greatest storm to hit Ireland in the past five hundred years was the hurricane that struck on the night of 6 January 1839. Weather forecasting at that time was still in its infancy, although people who possessed a barometer in their houses would have seen an extremely sharp drop in atmospheric pressure. A rapidly deepening depression in the North Atlantic tracked across Ireland, with pressure as low as 918–920 hPa. It passed rapidly over Ireland in about eight to nine hours, causing huge damage to property. The occasion would be referred to, for many years after, as Oíche na Gaoithe Móire, or 'the Night of the Big Wind'.

The west of Ireland was particularly vulnerable given that, in pre-Famine days, the houses were very flimsy, some of which were built with mud walls and most of which had thatched roofs. Initial fatalities were estimated at over five hundred, but the number was probably even higher, since bone and head injuries at the time generally ended in eventual death. People

The Corvette Galathea *in a Storm in the North Sea* by C.W. Eckersberg, 1839.

had to crawl along the ground to reach neighbours whose houses had been destroyed, and they were forced to use sign language to communicate as their voices could not be heard over the roaring of the storm-force winds. Superstitious people believed the storm was caused by 'the fairies', while more religious people feared that the end of the world was near.

In Dublin, one house in every four was damaged structurally, many of which lost their roofs. Several churches in the city opened their doors to shelter people, although the churches themselves sustained damage. A workhouse in Dorset Street was burnt out when the fire, which had initially been extinguished, was reignited by the winds. A small weaving industry in the Dublin Mountains was completely destroyed, as were the weavers' cottages. Up to ninety fishermen were lost in the sea off Skerries, while a stable wall that collapsed killed nine dray-horses in the Guinness brewery.

In 1908 the Old Age Pensions Act was introduced for people over seventy. This followed the 1863 Registration of Births and Deaths Act. Since many poor Catholics had never been registered at birth, one of the questions used to establish age was 'Can you remember the Night of the Big Wind?'

Oscar Wilde

The following moving children's story from *The Happy Prince and Other Tales* (1888) by Oscar Wilde (1854–1900) was told by Wilde to his own young sons. In Merrion Square, Dublin, today, a playground has been built which mirrors the theme of the story. Wilde and his parents once lived at 1 Merrion Square, having moved there from Westland Row. The building is now Oscar Wilde House. In 1997 J.D. Murphy and other members of the Oscar Wilde Society replaced one of the windows of 1 Merrion Square with a stained-glass image of 'the Happy Prince'. In the park also is the Danny Osborne statue of Oscar Wilde himself.

Oscar Wilde, *c.*1882.

The Selfish Giant

Every afternoon, as they were coming from school, the children used to go and play in the Giant's garden.

It was a large lovely garden, with soft green grass. Here and there over the grass stood beautiful flowers like stars, and there were twelve peach-trees that in the spring-time broke out into delicate blossoms of pink and pearl, and in the autumn bore rich fruit. The birds sat on the trees and sang so sweetly that the children used to stop their games in order to listen to them. 'How happy we are here!' they cried to each other.

One day the Giant came back. ...

'What are you doing here?' he cried in a very gruff voice, and the children ran away.

'My own garden is my own garden,' said the Giant; 'anyone can understand that, and I will allow nobody to play in it but myself.' So he built a high wall all round it, and put up a notice-board.

TRESPASSERS
WILL BE
PROSECUTED

Illustration for 'The Selfish Giant' by Walter Crane.

He was a very selfish Giant.

The poor children had now nowhere to play. They tried to play on the road, but the road was very dusty and full of hard stones, and they did not like it. They used to wander round the high wall when their lessons were over, and talk about the beautiful garden inside. 'How happy we were there,' they said to each other.

Then the Spring came, and all over the country there were little blossoms and little birds. Only in the garden of the Selfish Giant it was still Winter. The birds did not care to sing in it as there were no children, and the trees forgot to blossom. Once a beautiful flower put its head out from the grass, but when it saw the notice-board it was so sorry for the children that it slipped back into the ground again, and went off to sleep. ...

'I cannot understand why the Spring is so late in coming,' said the Selfish Giant, as he sat at the window and looked out at his cold white garden; 'I hope there will be a change in the weather.'

But the Spring never came, nor the Summer. The Autumn gave golden fruit to every garden, but to the Giant's garden she gave none. 'He is too selfish,' she said. So it was always Winter there, and the North Wind, and the Hail, and the Frost, and the Snow danced about through the trees.

One morning the Giant was lying awake in bed when he heard some lovely music. It sounded so sweet to his ears that he thought it must be the King's musicians passing by. It was really only a little linnet singing outside his window, but it was so long since he had heard a bird sing in his garden that it seemed to him to be the most beautiful music in the world. Then the Hail stopped dancing over his head, and the North Wind ceased roaring, and a delicious perfume came to him through the open casement. 'I believe the Spring has come at last,' said the Giant; and he jumped out of bed and looked out. What did he see?

He saw a most wonderful sight. Through a little hole in the wall the children had crept in, and they were sitting in the branches of the trees. In every tree that he could see there was a little child. And the trees were so glad to have the children back again that they had covered themselves with blossoms, and were waving their arms gently above the children's heads. The birds were flying about and twittering with delight, and the flowers were looking up through the green grass and laughing. It was a lovely scene, only in one corner it was still Winter. It was the farthest corner of the garden, and in it was standing a little boy. He was so small that he could not reach up to the branches of the tree, and he was wandering all round it, crying bitterly. The poor tree was still quite covered with frost and snow, and the North Wind was blowing and roaring above it. 'Climb up! little boy,' said the Tree, and it bent its branches down as low as it could; but the little boy was too tiny.

And the Giant's heart melted as he looked out. 'How selfish I have been!' he said; 'now I know why the Spring would not come here. I will put that poor little boy on the top of the tree, and then I will knock down the wall, and my garden shall be the children's playground for ever and ever.' He was really very sorry for what he had done.

So he crept downstairs and opened the front door quite softly, and went out into the garden. But when the children saw him they were so frightened that they all ran away, and the garden became Winter again. Only the little boy did not run, for his eyes were so full of tears that he did not see the Giant coming. And the Giant stole up behind him and took him gently in his hand, and put him up into the tree. And the tree broke at once into blossom, and the birds came and sang on it, and the little boy stretched out his two arms and flung them round the Giant's neck, and kissed him. And the other children, when they saw that the Giant was not wicked any longer, came running back, and with them came the Spring. 'It is your garden now, little children,' said the Giant, and he took a great axe and knocked down the wall. And when the people were going to market at twelve o'clock they found the Giant playing with the children in the most beautiful garden they had ever seen.

All day long they played, and in the evening they came to the Giant to bid him good-bye.

'But where is your little companion?' he said: 'the boy I put into the tree.' The Giant loved him the best because he had kissed him.

'We don't know,' answered the children; 'he has gone away.'

'You must tell him to be sure and come here to-morrow,' said the Giant. But the children said that they did not know where he lived, and had never seen him before; and the Giant felt very sad.

Every afternoon, when school was over, the children came and played with the Giant. But the little boy whom the Giant loved was never seen again. The Giant was very kind to all the children, yet he longed for his first little friend, and often spoke of him. 'How I would like to see him!' he used to say.

Years went over, and the Giant grew very old and feeble. ...

One winter morning he looked out of his window as he was dressing. He did not hate the Winter now, for he knew that it was merely the Spring asleep, and that the flowers were resting.

Suddenly he rubbed his eyes in wonder, and looked and looked. It certainly was a marvellous sight. In the farthest corner of the garden was a tree quite covered with lovely white blossoms. Its branches were all golden, and silver fruit hung down from them, and underneath it stood the little boy he had loved.

Downstairs ran the Giant in great joy, and out into the garden. He hastened across the grass, and came near to the child. And when he came quite close his face grew red with anger, and he said, 'Who hath dared to wound thee?' For on the palms of the child's hands were the prints of

two nails, and the prints of two nails were on the little feet.

Cherry blossom, Phoenix Park.

'Who hath dared to wound thee?' cried the Giant; 'tell me, that I may take my big sword and slay him.'

'Nay!' answered the child; 'but these are the wounds of Love.'

'Who art thou?' said the Giant, and a strange awe fell on him, and he knelt before the little child.

And the child smiled on the Giant, and said to him, 'You let me play once in your garden, to-day you shall come with me to my garden, which is Paradise.'

And when the children ran in that afternoon, they found the Giant lying dead under the tree, all covered with white blossoms.

CHAPTER 4

The Seventh City of Christendom – Joyce's Dublin

The world of Joyce's novels rarely focuses on the poverty and squalor experienced by Dublin's inner-city population, yet neither does it focus on the lives of the wealthy, largely Protestant commercial class. From *Ulysses* to *Dubliners* to *A Portrait of the Artist as a Young Man*, the reader becomes familiar with lower-middle-class characters, better-off Catholics who are still 'shabby genteel' in comparison to their Protestant neighbours. Joycean Dublin was a city divided: its inner-city inhabitants lived in overcrowded and unsanitary conditions while their more affluent neighbours lived in the wealthier suburbs which had sprung up at the turn of the twentieth century, often renting tenements to the poor. The literary works of Sean O'Casey, and later of James Plunkett, would capture this world more strikingly, yet Joyce did reflect the politics of the times and, more importantly, the eternal human condition.

James Joyce by Adolf Hoffmeister, 1966.

Sackville Street
(O'Connell Street),
1893.

Dubliners

The following extract is from the short story 'The Dead', from Joyce's collection *Dubliners* (1914). Here the protagonist, Gabriel Conroy, returns with his wife, Gretta, to the Gresham Hotel having been to a festive evening in Usher's Island, Dublin. He is looking forward to a romantic interlude. Gretta is silent and preoccupied, however. When Gabriel presses her, she reveals that she is sad because she recalls a young man who was once in love with her, years before, in Galway. After she cries herself to sleep Gabriel has to contend with the spirit of that young man, Michael Furey. He must re-evaluate the entire nature of his own relationship with Gretta. 'The Dead' is considered a masterpiece of the short-story form. In 1987 John Huston directed the film version of the short story, starring Donal McCann as Gabriel Conroy and Anjelica Huston as Gretta. It was the last film that Huston directed before his death that same year.

From 'The Dead'

An old man was dozing in a great hooded chair in the hall. He lit a candle in the office and went before them to the stairs. They followed him in silence, their feet falling in soft thuds on the thickly carpeted stairs. ...

The porter led them along a corridor and opened a door. Then he set his unstable candle down on a toilet-table and asked at what hour they were to be called in the morning.

'Eight,' said Gabriel.

The porter pointed to the tap of the electric-light and began a muttered apology, but Gabriel cut him short. 'We don't want any light. We have light enough from the street. And I say,' he added, pointing to the candle, 'you might remove that handsome article, like a good man.' The porter took up his candle again, but slowly, for he was surprised by such a novel idea. Then he mumbled good-night and went out. Gabriel shot the lock to. A ghastly light from the street lamp lay in a long shaft from one window to the door. Gabriel threw his overcoat and hat on a couch and crossed the room towards the window. He looked down into the street in order that his emotion might calm a little. Then he turned and leaned against a chest of drawers with his back to the light. She had taken off her hat and cloak and was standing before a large swinging mirror, unhooking her waist. Gabriel paused for a few moments, watching her, and then said: 'Gretta!' She turned away from the mirror slowly and walked along the shaft of light towards him. Her face looked so serious and weary that the words would not pass Gabriel's lips. No, it was not the moment yet.

'You looked tired,' he said. 'I am a little,' she answered. 'You don't feel ill or weak?' 'No, tired: that's all.' She went on to the window and stood there, looking out. Gabriel waited again and then, fearing that diffidence was about to conquer him, he said abruptly: 'By the way, Gretta!'

'What is it?' 'You know that poor fellow Malins?' he said quickly. 'Yes. What about him?' 'Well, poor fellow, he's a decent sort of chap, after all,' continued Gabriel in a false voice. 'He gave me back that sovereign I lent him,

Henry Street.

and I didn't expect it, really. It's a pity he wouldn't keep away from that Browne, because he's not a bad fellow, really.' He was trembling now with annoyance. Why did she seem so abstracted? He did not know how he could begin. Was she annoyed, too, about something? If she would only turn to him or come to him of her own accord! To take her as she was would be brutal. No, he must see some ardour in her eyes first. He longed to be master of her strange mood. 'When did you lend him the pound?' she asked, after a pause. Gabriel strove to restrain himself from breaking out into brutal language about the sottish Malins and his pound. He longed to cry to her from his soul, to crush her body against his, to overmaster her. But he said: 'O, at Christmas, when he opened that little Christmas-card shop in Henry Street.' He was in such a fever of rage and desire that he did not hear her come from the window. She stood before him for an instant, looking at him strangely. Then, suddenly raising herself on tiptoe and resting her hands lightly on his shoulders, she kissed him. 'You are a very generous person, Gabriel,' she said. Gabriel, trembling with delight at her sudden kiss and at the quaintness of her phrase, put his hands on her hair and began smoothing it back, scarcely touching it with his fingers. The washing had made it fine and brilliant. His heart was brimming over with happiness. Just when he was wishing for it she had come to him of her own accord. Perhaps her thoughts had been running with his. Perhaps she had felt the impetuous desire that was in him, and then the yielding mood had come upon her. Now that she had fallen to him so easily, he wondered why he had been so diffident. He stood, holding her head between his hands. Then, slipping one arm swiftly about her body and drawing her towards him, he said

James Joyce House, where 'The Dead' is set.

softly: 'Gretta, dear, what are you thinking about?' She did not answer nor yield wholly to his arm. He said again, softly: 'Tell me what it is, Gretta. I think I know what is the matter. Do I know?' She did not answer at once. Then she said in an outburst of tears: 'O, I am thinking about that song, The Lass of Aughrim.' She broke loose from him and ran to the bed and, throwing her arms across the bed-rail, hid her face. Gabriel stood stock-still for a moment in astonishment and then followed her. As he passed in the way of the cheval-glass he caught sight of himself in full length, his broad, well-filled shirt-front, the face whose expression always puzzled him when he saw it in a mirror, and his glimmering gilt-rimmed eyeglasses. He halted a few paces from her and said: 'What about the song? Why does that make you cry?' She raised her head from her arms and dried her eyes with the back of her hand like a child. A kinder note than he had intended went into his voice. 'Why, Gretta?' he asked. 'I am thinking about a person long ago who used to sing that song.' 'And who was the person long ago?' asked Gabriel, smiling. 'It was a person I used to know in Galway when I was living with my grandmother,' she said.

The smile passed away from Gabriel's face. A dull anger began to gather again at the back of his mind and the dull fires of his lust began to glow angrily in his veins. 'Someone you were in love with?' he asked ironically. 'It was a young boy I used to know,' she answered, 'named Michael Furey. He used to sing that song, The Lass of Aughrim. He was very delicate.' Gabriel was silent. He did not wish her to think that he was interested in this delicate boy. 'I can see him so plainly,' she said, after a moment. 'Such eyes as he had: big, dark eyes! And such an expression in them – an expression!' 'O, then, you are in love with him?' said Gabriel. 'I used to go out walking with him,' she said, 'when I was in Galway.' A thought flew across Gabriel's mind. 'Perhaps that was why you wanted to go to Galway with that Ivors girl?' he said coldly. She looked at him and asked in surprise: 'What for?' Her eyes made Gabriel feel awkward. He shrugged his shoulders and said: 'How do I know? To see him, perhaps.' She looked away from him along the shaft of light towards the window in silence. 'He is dead,' she said at length. 'He died when he was only seventeen. Isn't it a terrible thing to die so young as that?' 'What was he?' asked Gabriel, still ironically. 'He was in the gasworks,' she said. Gabriel felt humiliated by the failure of his irony and by the evocation of this figure from the dead, a boy in the gasworks. While he had been full of memories of their secret life together, full of tenderness and joy and desire, she had been comparing him in her mind with another. A shameful consciousness of his own person assailed him. He saw himself as a ludicrous figure, acting as a pennyboy for his aunts, a nervous, well-meaning sentimentalist, orating to vulgarians and idealising his own clownish lusts, the pitiable fatuous fellow he had caught a glimpse of in the mirror. Instinctively he turned his back more to the light lest she might see the shame that burned upon his forehead. He tried to keep up his tone of cold interrogation, but his voice when he spoke was humble and indifferent. 'I suppose you were in love with this Michael Furey, Gretta,' he said. 'I was great with him at that time,' she said.[1] Her voice was veiled and sad. Gabriel, feeling now how vain it would be to

1 'Great with': from the Irish *mór leis*, meaning 'very close to'.

try to lead her whither he had purposed, caressed one of her hands and said, also sadly: 'And what did he die of so young, Gretta? Consumption, was it?' 'I think he died for me,' she answered. A vague terror seized Gabriel at this answer, as if, at that hour when he had hoped to triumph, some impalpable and vindictive being was coming against him, gathering forces against him in its vague world. But he shook himself free of it with an effort of reason and continued to caress her hand. He did not question her again, for he felt that she would tell him of herself. Her hand was warm and moist: it did not respond to his touch, but he continued to caress it just as he had caressed her first letter to him that spring morning. 'It was in the winter,' she said, 'about the beginning of the winter when I was going to leave my grandmother's and come up here to the convent. And he was ill at the time in his lodgings in Galway and wouldn't be let out, and his people in Oughterard were written to. He was in decline, they said, or something like that. I never knew rightly.' She paused for a moment and sighed. 'Poor fellow,' she said. 'He was very fond of me and he was such a gentle boy. We used to go out together, walking, you know, Gabriel, like the way they do in the country. He was going to study singing only for his health. He had a very good voice, poor Michael Furey.' 'Well; and then?' asked Gabriel. 'And then when it came to the time for me to leave Galway and come up to the convent he was much worse and I wouldn't be let see him so I wrote him a letter saying I was going up to Dublin and would be back in the summer, and hoping he would be better then.' She paused for a moment to get her voice under control, and then went on: 'Then the night before I left, I was in my grandmother's house in Nuns' Island, packing up, and I heard gravel thrown up against the window. The window was so wet I couldn't see, so I ran downstairs as I was and slipped out the back into the garden and there was the poor fellow at the end of the garden, shivering.' 'And

Connolly Station.

did you not tell him to go back?' asked Gabriel. 'I implored of him to go home at once and told him he would get his death in the rain. But he said he did not want to live. I can see his eyes as well as well! He was standing at the end of the wall where there was a tree.' 'And did he go home?' asked Gabriel. 'Yes, he went home. And when I was only a week in the convent he died and he was buried in Oughterard, where his people came from. O, the day I heard that, that he was dead!'

She stopped, choking with sobs, and, overcome by emotion, flung herself face downward on the bed, sobbing in the quilt. Gabriel held her hand for a moment longer, irresolutely, and then, shy of intruding on her grief, let it fall gently and walked quietly to the window. She was fast asleep. Gabriel, leaning on his elbow, looked for a few moments unresentfully on her tangled hair and half-open mouth, listening to her deep-drawn breath. So she had had that romance in her life: a man had died for her sake. It hardly pained him now to think how poor a part he, her husband, had played in her life. He watched her while she slept, as though he and she had never lived together as man and wife. His curious eyes rested long upon her face and on her hair: and, as he thought of what she must have been then, in that time of her first girlish beauty, a strange, friendly pity for her entered his soul. He did not like to say even to himself that her face was no longer beautiful, but he knew that it was no longer the face for which Michael Furey had braved death. Perhaps she had not told him all the story. His eyes moved to the chair over which she had thrown some of her clothes. A petticoat string dangled to the floor. One boot stood upright, its limp upper fallen down: the fellow of it lay upon its side. He wondered at his riot of emotions of an hour before. From what had it proceeded? From his aunt's supper, from his own foolish speech, from the wine and dancing, the merry-making when saying good-night in the hall, the pleasure of the walk along the river in the snow. Poor Aunt Julia! She, too, would soon be a shade with the shade of Patrick Morkan and his horse. He had caught that haggard look upon her face for a moment when she was singing Arrayed for the Bridal. Soon, perhaps, he would be sitting in that same drawing-room, dressed in black, his silk hat on his knees. The blinds would be drawn down and Aunt Kate would be sitting beside him, crying and blowing her nose and telling him how Julia had died. He would cast about in his mind for some words that might console her, and would find only lame and useless ones. Yes, yes: that would happen very soon. The air of the room chilled his shoulders. He stretched himself cautiously along under the sheets and lay down beside his wife. One by one, they were all becoming shades. Better pass boldly into that other world, in the full glory of some passion, than fade and wither dismally with age. He thought of how she who lay beside him had locked in her heart for so many years that image of her lover's eyes when he had told her that he did not wish to live. Generous tears filled Gabriel's eyes. He had never felt like that himself towards any woman, but he knew that such a feeling must be love. The tears gathered more thickly in his eyes and in the partial darkness he imagined he saw the form of a young man standing under a dripping tree.

Other forms were near. His soul had approached that region where dwell the vast hosts of the dead. He was conscious of, but could not apprehend, their wayward and flickering existence. His own identity was fading out into a grey impalpable world: the solid world itself, which these dead had one time reared and lived in, was dissolving and dwindling.

A few light taps upon the pane made him turn to the window. It had begun to snow again. He watched sleepily the flakes, silver and dark, falling obliquely against the lamplight. The time had come for him to set out on his journey westward. Yes, the newspapers were right: snow was general all over Ireland. It was falling on every part of the dark central plain, on the treeless hills, falling softly upon the Bog of Allen and, farther westward, softly falling into the dark mutinous Shannon waves. It was falling, too, upon every part of the lonely churchyard on the hill where Michael Furey lay buried. It lay thickly drifted on the crooked crosses and headstones, on the spears of the little gate, on the barren thorns. His soul swooned slowly as he heard the snow falling faintly through the universe and faintly falling, like the descent of their last end, upon all the living and the dead.

A Portrait of the Artist as a Young Man

The following extract is from *A Portrait of the Artist as a Young Man*. The protagonist, Stephen Dedalus, has considered a religious vocation, having repented of his licentious life. While by the sea at Dollymount Strand in Dublin, however, he sees a vision of his namesake, Daedalus, the great artificer, and is moved by the beauty of a girl standing in the water. In this epiphanic moment, he realises that his real vocation is to be an artist and that, as a writer, he will go on to record the beauty of the world: 'to live, to err, to fall, to triumph, to recreate life out of life!'

An Epiphany on Dollymount Strand

He turned seaward from the road at Dollymount and as he passed on to the thin wooden bridge he felt the planks shaking with the tramp of heavily shod feet. A squad of Christian Brothers was on its way back from the Bull and had begun to pass, two by two, across the bridge. Soon the whole bridge was trembling and resounding. The uncouth faces passed him two by two, stained yellow or red or livid by the sea, and, as he strove to look at them with ease and indifference, a faint stain of personal shame and commiseration rose to his own face. Angry with himself he tried to hide his face from their eyes by gazing down sideways into the shallow swirling water under the bridge but he still saw a reflection therein of their top-heavy silk hats and humble tape-like collars and loosely-hanging clerical clothes.

　　—Brother Hickey.
　　Brother Quaid.
　　Brother MacArdle.
　　Brother Keogh.—

Their piety would be like their names, like their faces, like their clothes, and it was idle for him to tell himself that their humble and contrite hearts, it might be, paid a far richer tribute of devotion than his had ever been, a gift tenfold more acceptable than his elaborate adoration. ...

He drew forth a phrase from his treasure and spoke it softly to himself:

—A day of dappled seaborne clouds.

The phrase and the day and the scene harmonized in a chord. Words. Was it their colours? He allowed them to glow and fade, hue after hue: sunrise gold, the russet and green of apple orchards, azure of waves, the grey-fringed fleece of clouds. No, it was not their colours: it was the poise and balance of the period itself. Did he then love the rhythmic rise and fall of words better than their associations of legend and colour? Or was it that, being as weak of sight as he was shy of mind, he drew less pleasure from the reflection of the glowing sensible world through the prism of a language many-coloured and richly storied than from the contemplation of an inner world of individual emotions mirrored perfectly in a lucid supple periodic prose? ...

A veiled sunlight lit up faintly the grey sheet of water where the river was embayed. In the distance along the

Dollymount Strand.

course of the slow-flowing Liffey slender masts flecked the sky and, more distant still, the dim fabric of the city lay prone in haze. Like a scene on some vague arras, old as man's weariness, the image of the seventh city of christendom was visible to him across the timeless air, no older nor more weary nor less patient of subjection than in the days of the thingmote.

Disheartened, he raised his eyes towards the slow-drifting clouds, dappled and seaborne. They were voyaging across the deserts of the sky, a host of nomads on the march, voyaging high over Ireland, westward bound. The Europe they had come from lay out there beyond the Irish Sea, Europe of strange tongues and valleyed and woodbegirt and citadelled and of entrenched and marshalled races.

Again! Again! Again! A voice from beyond the world was calling.

—Hello, Stephanos!

—Here comes The Dedalus!

—Ao! Eh, give it over, Dwyer, I'm telling you, or I'll give you a stuff in the kisser for yourself. Ao!

—Good man, Towser! Duck him!

—Come along, Dedalus! Bous Stephanoumenos! Bous Stephaneforos!

—Duck him! Guzzle him now, Towser!

—Help! Help! Ao!

He recognized their speech collectively before he distinguished their faces. The mere sight of that medley of wet nakedness chilled him to the bone. Their bodies, corpse-white or suffused with a pallid golden light or rawly tanned by the sun, gleamed with the wet of the sea. ...

He stood still in deference to their calls and parried their banter with easy words. ...

Their banter was not new to him and now it flattered his mild proud sovereignty. Now, as never before, his strange name

Dublin Bay in the late nineteenth century.

seemed to him a prophecy. So timeless seemed the grey warm air, so fluid and impersonal his own mood, that all ages were as one to him. A moment before the ghost of the ancient kingdom of the Danes had looked forth through the vesture of the hazewrapped city. Now, at the name of the fabulous artificer, he seemed to hear the noise of dim waves and to see a winged form flying above the waves and slowly climbing the air. What did it mean? Was it a quaint device opening a page of some medieval book of prophecies and symbols, a hawk-like man flying sunward above the sea, a prophecy of the end he had been born to serve and had been following through the mists of childhood and boyhood, a symbol of the artist forging anew in his workshop out of the sluggish matter of the earth a new soaring impalpable imperishable being?

His heart trembled; his breath came faster and a wild spirit passed over his limbs as though he was soaring sunward. His heart trembled in an ecstasy of fear and his soul was in flight. His soul was soaring in an air beyond the world and the body he knew was purified in a breath and delivered of incertitude and made radiant and commingled with the element of the spirit. An ecstasy of flight made radiant his eyes and wild his breath and tremulous and wild and radiant his windswept limbs.

—One! Two! Look out!

—Oh, Cripes, I'm drownded!

—One! Two! Three and away!

—The next! The next!

—One! UK!

—Stephaneforos!

His throat ached with a desire to cry aloud, the cry of a hawk or eagle on high, to cry piercingly of his deliverance to the winds. This was the call of life to his soul not the dull gross voice of the world of duties and despair, not the inhuman voice that had called him to the pale service of the altar. An instant of wild flight had delivered him and the cry of triumph which his lips withheld cleft his brain.

—Stephaneforos!

What were they now but cerements shaken from the body of death – the fear he had walked in night and day, the incertitude that had ringed him round, the shame that had abased him within and without – cerements, the linens of the grave? His soul had arisen from the grave of boyhood, spurning her grave-clothes. Yes! Yes! Yes! He would create proudly out of the freedom and power of his soul, as the great artificer whose name he bore, a living thing, new and soaring and beautiful, impalpable, imperishable. ...

He looked northward towards Howth. The sea had fallen below the line of seawrack on the shallow side of the breakwater and already the tide was running out fast along the foreshore. Already one long oval bank of sand lay warm and dry amid the wavelets. Here and there warm isles of sand gleamed above the shallow tide and about the isles and around the long bank and amid the shallow currents of the beach were lightclad figures, wading and delving.

In a few moments he was barefoot, his stockings folded in his pockets and his canvas shoes dangling by their knotted laces over his shoulders and, picking a pointed salt-eaten stick out of the jetsam among the rocks, he clambered down the slope of the breakwater. ...

Where was his boyhood now? Where was the soul that had hung back from her destiny, to brood alone upon the shame of her wounds and in her house of squalor and subterfuge to queen it in faded cerements and in wreaths that withered at the touch? Or where was he?

He was alone. He was unheeded, happy and near to the wild heart of life. He was alone and young and wilful and wildhearted, alone amid a waste of wild air and brackish waters and the sea-harvest of shells and tangle and veiled grey sunlight and gayclad lightclad figures of children and girls and voices childish and girlish in the air.

Howth Head from Dollymount Strand.

A girl stood before him in midstream, alone and still, gazing out to sea. She seemed like one whom magic had changed into the likeness of a strange and beautiful seabird. Her long slender bare legs were delicate as a crane's and pure save where an emerald trail of seaweed had fashioned itself as a sign upon the flesh. Her thighs, fuller and soft-hued as ivory, were bared almost to the hips, where the white fringes of her drawers were like feathering of soft white down. Her slate-blue skirts were kilted boldly about her waist and dovetailed behind her. Her bosom was as a bird's, soft and slight, slight and soft as the breast of some dark-plumaged dove. But her long fair hair was girlish: and girlish, and touched with the wonder of mortal beauty, her face.

She was alone and still, gazing out to sea; and when she felt his presence and the worship of his eyes her eyes turned to him in quiet sufferance of his gaze, without shame or wantonness. Long, long she suffered his gaze and then quietly withdrew her eyes from his and bent them towards the stream, gently stirring the water with her foot hither and thither. The first faint noise of gently moving water broke the silence, low and faint and whispering, faint as the bells of sleep; hither and thither, hither and thither; and a faint flame trembled on her cheek.

—Heavenly God! cried Stephen's soul, in an outburst of profane joy.

He turned away from her suddenly and set off across the strand. His cheeks were aflame; his body was aglow; his limbs were trembling. On and on and on and on he strode, far out over the sands, singing wildly to the sea, crying to greet the advent of the life that had cried to him.

Her image had passed into his soul for ever and no word had broken the holy silence of his ecstasy. Her eyes had called him and his soul had leaped at the call. To live, to err, to fall, to triumph, to recreate life out of life! A wild angel had appeared to him, the angel of mortal youth and beauty, an envoy from the fair courts of life, to throw open before him in an instant of ecstasy the gates of all the ways of error and glory. On and on and on and on!

He halted suddenly and heard his heart in the silence. How far had he walked? What hour was it?

There was no human figure near him nor any sound borne to him over the air. But the tide was near the turn and already the day was on the wane. He turned landward and ran towards the shore and, running up the sloping beach, reckless of the sharp shingle, found a sandy nook amid a ring of tufted sandknolls and lay down there that the peace and silence of the evening might still the riot of his blood.

He felt above him the vast indifferent dome and the calm processes of the heavenly bodies; and the earth beneath him, the earth that had borne him, had taken him to her breast.

He closed his eyes in the languor of sleep. ...

Evening had fallen when he woke and the sand and arid grasses of his bed glowed no longer. He rose slowly and, recalling the rapture of his sleep, sighed at its joy.

Ulysses

In the following extract from Joyce's *Ulysses* the central character, Leopold Bloom, leaves his house in Eccles Street and goes out to the butcher's to buy a kidney and prepare breakfast for his wife Marion (Molly) who is still in bed. A letter arrives for her, and Bloom suspects it is from Blazes Boylan, her tour manager and possible lover. (Molly is a trained singer.) Bloom reads a letter from his fifteen-year-old daughter, Milly. She has also sent her mother a card from Mullingar where she is staying. In the Homeric parallel, the nymph Calypso kept Odysseus in amorous captivity for seven years on the island of Ogygia. Here Molly keeps Bloom in amorous captivity despite her infidelity.

From Chapter 4 – 'Calypso'

Mr Leopold Bloom ate with relish the inner organs of beasts and fowls. He liked thick giblet soup, nutty gizzards, a stuffed roast heart, liverslices fried with crustcrumbs, fried hencods' roes. Most of all he liked grilled mutton kidneys which gave to his palate a fine tang of faintly scented urine. ...

The coals were reddening.

Another slice of bread and butter: three, four: right. She didn't like her plate full. Right. He turned from the tray, lifted the kettle off the hob and set it sideways on the fire. It sat there, dull and squat, its spout stuck out. Cup of tea soon. Good. Mouth dry. The cat walked stiffly round a leg of the table with tail on high.

—Mkgnao!

—O, there you are, Mr Bloom said, turning from the fire.

The cat mewed in answer and stalked again stiffly round a leg of the table, mewing. Just how she stalks over my writingtable. Prr. Scratch my head. Prr.

Mr Bloom watched curiously, kindly the lithe black form. Clean to see: the gloss of her sleek hide, the white button under the butt of her tail, the green flashing eyes. He bent down to her, his hands on his knees.

—Milk for the pussens, he said.

—Mrkgnao! the cat cried.

They call them stupid. They understand what we say better than we understand them. She understands all

Grafton Street.

she wants to. Vindictive too. Cruel. Her nature. Curious mice never squeal. Seem to like it. Wonder what I look like to her. Height of a tower? No, she can jump me.

—Afraid of the chickens she is, he said mockingly. Afraid of the chookchooks. I never saw such a stupid pussens as the pussens.

—Mrkrgnao! the cat said loudly. ...

—Gurrhr! she cried, running to lap.

He watched the bristles shining wirily in the weak light as she tipped three times and licked lightly. Wonder is it true if you clip them they can't mouse after. Why? They shine in the dark, perhaps, the tips. Or kind of feelers in the dark, perhaps. ...

On quietly creaky boots he went up the staircase to the hall, paused by the bedroom door. She might like something tasty. Thin bread and butter she likes in the morning. Still perhaps: once in a way.

He said softly in the bare hall:

—I'm going round the corner. Be back in a minute.

And when he had heard his voice say it he added:

—You don't want anything for breakfast?

A sleepy soft grunt answered:

—Mn.

No. She didn't want anything. He heard then a warm heavy sigh, softer, as she turned over and the loose brass quoits of the bedstead jingled. Must get those settled really. Pity. All the way from Gibraltar. Forgotten any little Spanish she knew. ...

His hand took his hat from the peg over his initialled heavy overcoat and his lost property office secondhand waterproof. Stamps: stickyback pictures. Daresay lots of officers are in the swim too. Course they do. The sweated legend in the crown of his hat told him mutely: Plasto's high grade ha. He peeped quickly inside the leather headband. White slip of paper. Quite safe.

On the doorstep he felt in his hip pocket for the latchkey. Not there. In the trousers I left off. Must get it. Potato I have. Creaky wardrobe. No use disturbing her. She turned over sleepily that time. He pulled the halldoor to after him very quietly, more, till the footleaf dropped gently over the threshold, a limp lid. Looked shut. All right till I come back anyhow.

He crossed to the bright side, avoiding the loose cellarflap of number seventyfive. ...

A girl playing one of those instruments what do you call them: dulcimers. I pass.

Probably not a bit like it really. Kind of stuff you read: in the track of the sun. Sunburst on the titlepage. He smiled, pleasing himself. What Arthur Griffith said about the headpiece over the *Freeman* leader: a homerule sun rising up in the northwest from the laneway behind the bank of Ireland. He prolonged his pleased smile. Ikey touch that: homerule sun rising up in the northwest. ...

Baldhead over the blind. Cute old codger. No use canvassing him for an ad. Still he knows his own business best. There he is, sure enough, my bold Larry, leaning against the sugarbin in his shirtsleeves watching the aproned curate swab up with mop and bucket. Simon Dedalus takes him off to a tee with his eyes screwed up. Do you know what I'm going to tell you? What's that, Mr O'Rourke? Do you know what? The Russians, they'd only be an eight o'clock breakfast for the Japanese.

Stop and say a word: about the funeral perhaps. Sad thing about poor Dignam, Mr O'Rourke.

Turning into Dorset street he said freshly in greeting through the doorway:

—Good day, Mr O'Rourke.

—Good day to you.

—Lovely weather, sir.

—'Tis all that. ...

He halted before Dlugacz's window, staring at the hanks of sausages, polonies, black and white. Fifteen multiplied by. The figures whitened in his mind, unsolved: displeased, he let them fade. The shiny links, packed with forcemeat, fed his gaze and he breathed in tranquilly the lukewarm breath of cooked spicy pigs' blood.

A kidney oozed bloodgouts on the willowpatterned dish: the last. He stood by the nextdoor girl at the counter.

Would she buy it too, calling the items from a slip in her hand? Chapped: washingsoda. And a pound and a half of Denny's sausages. His eyes rested on her vigorous hips. Woods his name is. Wonder what he does. Wife is oldish. New blood. No followers allowed. Strong pair of arms. Whacking a carpet on the clothesline. She does whack it, by George. The way her crooked skirt swings at each whack.

The ferreteyed porkbutcher folded the sausages he had snipped off with blotchy fingers, sausagepink. Sound meat there: like a stallfed heifer. ...

The porkbutcher snapped two sheets from the pile, wrapped up her prime sausages and made a red grimace.

—Now, my miss, he said.

She tendered a coin, smiling boldly, holding her thick wrist out.

—Thank you, my miss. And one shilling threepence change. For you, please?

Mr Bloom pointed quickly. To catch up and walk behind her if she went slowly, behind her moving hams. Pleasant to see first thing in the morning. Hurry up, damn it. Make hay while the sun shines. She stood

British penny, 1904.

outside the shop in sunlight and sauntered lazily to the right. He sighed down his nose: they never understand. Sodachapped hands. Crusted toenails too. Brown scapulars in tatters, defending her both ways. The sting of disregard glowed to weak pleasure within his breast. For another: a constable off duty cuddling her in Eccles Lane. They like them sizeable. Prime sausage. O please, Mr Policeman, I'm lost in the wood.

—Threepence, please.

His hand accepted the moist tender gland and slid it into a sidepocket. Then it fetched up three coins from his trousers' pocket and laid them on the rubber prickles. They lay, were read quickly and quickly slid, disc by disc, into the till.

—Thank you, sir. Another time.

A speck of eager fire from foxeyes thanked him. He withdrew his gaze after an instant. No: better not: another time.

—Good morning, he said, moving away.

—Good morning, sir.

No sign. Gone. What matter?

He walked back along Dorset street. ...

Desolation. ...

Quick warm sunlight came running from Berkeley road, swiftly, in slim sandals, along the brightening footpath. Runs, she runs to meet me, a girl with gold hair on the wind.

Two letters and a card lay on the hallfloor. He stooped and gathered them. Mrs Marion Bloom. His quickened heart slowed at once. Bold hand. Mrs Marion.

—Poldy!

Entering the bedroom he halfclosed his eyes and walked through warm yellow twilight towards her tousled head.

—Who are the letters for?

He looked at them. Mullingar. Milly.

—A letter for me from Milly, he said carefully, and a card to you. And a letter for you.

He laid her card and letter on the twill bedspread near the curve of her knees.

—Do you want the blind up?

Letting the blind up by gentle tugs halfway his backward eye saw her glance at the letter and tuck it under her pillow.

—That do? he asked, turning.

She was reading the card, propped on her elbow.

—She got the things, she said.

He waited till she had laid the card aside and curled herself back slowly with a snug sigh.

—Hurry up with that tea, she said. I'm parched.

—The kettle is boiling, he said.

But he delayed to clear the chair: her striped petticoat, tossed soiled linen: and lifted all in an armful on to the foot of the bed.

Dorset Street, *c.*1913.
Reproduced courtesy of
the National Library of
Ireland.

As he went down the kitchen stairs she called:

—Poldy!

—What?

—Scald the teapot.

On the boil sure enough: a plume of steam from the spout. He scalded and rinsed out the teapot and put in four full spoons of tea, tilting the kettle then to let the water flow in. Having set it to draw he took off the kettle, crushed the pan flat on the live coals and watched the lump of butter slide and melt. While he unwrapped the kidney the cat mewed hungrily against him. Give her too much meat she won't mouse. Say they won't eat pork. Kosher. Here. He let the bloodsmeared paper fall to her and dropped the kidney amid the sizzling butter sauce. Pepper. He sprinkled it through his fingers ringwise from the chipped eggcup.

Then he slit open his letter, glancing down the page and over. Thanks: new tam: Mr Coghlan: lough Owel picnic: young student: Blazes Boylan's seaside girls.

The tea was drawn. He filled his own moustachecup, sham crown Derby, smiling. Silly Milly's birthday gift. Only five she was then. No, wait: four. I gave her the amberoid necklace she broke. Putting pieces of folded brown paper in the letterbox for her. ...

He prodded a fork into the kidney and slapped it over: then fitted the teapot on the tray. Its hump bumped as he took it up. Everything on it? Bread and butter, four, sugar, spoon, her cream. Yes. He carried it upstairs, his thumb hooked in the teapot handle.

Nudging the door open with his knee he carried the tray in and set it on the chair by the bedhead.

—What a time you were! she said.

She set the brasses jingling as she raised herself briskly, an elbow on the pillow. He looked calmly down on her bulk and between her large soft bubs, sloping within her nightdress like a shegoat's udder. The warmth of her couched body rose on the air, mingling with the fragrance of the tea she poured.

A strip of torn envelope peeped from under the dimpled pillow. In the act of going he stayed to straighten the bedspread.

—Who was the letter from? he asked.

Bold hand. Marion.

—O, Boylan, she said. He's bringing the programme.

—What are you singing?

—*Là ci darem* with J.C. Doyle, she said, and *Love's Old Sweet Song*.

Her full lips, drinking, smiled. Rather stale smell that incense leaves next day. Like foul flowerwater.

—Would you like the window open a little?

She doubled a slice of bread into her mouth, asking:

—What time is the funeral?

—Eleven, I think, he answered. I didn't see the paper.

Following the pointing of her finger he took up a leg of her soiled drawers from the bed. No? Then, a twisted grey garter looped round a stocking: rumpled, shiny sole.

—No: that book.

Other stocking. Her petticoat.

—It must have fell down, she said. ...

By prodding a prong of the fork under the kidney he detached it and turned it turtle on its back. Only a little burnt. He tossed it off the pan on to a plate and let the scanty brown gravy trickle over it.

Cup of tea now. He sat down, cut and buttered a slice of the loaf. He shore away the burnt flesh and flung it to the cat. Then he put a forkful into his mouth, chewing with discernment the toothsome pliant meat. Done to a turn. A mouthful of tea. Then he cut away dies of bread, sopped one in the gravy and put it in his mouth. What was that about some young student and a picnic? He creased out the letter at his side, reading it slowly as he chewed, sopping another die of bread in the gravy and raising it to his mouth.

Dearest Papli

Thanks ever so much for the lovely birthday present. It suits me splendid. Everyone says I am quite the belle in my new tam. I got mummy's lovely box of creams and am writing. They are lovely. I am getting on swimming in the photo business now. Mr Coghlan took one of me and Mrs. will send when developed. We did great biz yesterday. Fair day and all the beef to the heels were in. We are going to lough Owel on Monday with a few friends to make a scrap picnic. Give my love to mummy and to yourself a big kiss and thanks. I hear them at the piano downstairs. There is to be a concert in the Greville Arms on Saturday. There is a young student comes here some evenings named Bannon his cousins or something are big swells and he sings Boylan's (I was on the pop of writing Blazes Boylan's) song about those seaside girls. Tell him silly Milly sends my best respects. I must now close with fondest love

Your fond daughter,

Milly.

P.S. Excuse bad writing am in hurry. Byby.

M.

Fifteen yesterday. Curious, fifteenth of the month too. Her first birthday away from home. Separation. Remember the summer morning she was born, running to knock up Mrs Thornton in Denzille street. Jolly old woman. Lot of babies she must have helped into the world. She knew from the first poor little Rudy wouldn't live. Well, God is good, sir. She knew at once. He would be eleven now if he had lived. ...

Milly too. Young kisses: the first. Far away now past. Mrs Marion. Reading, lying back now, counting the strands of her hair, smiling, braiding.

Finnegans Wake

Finnegans Wake (1939) is a challenging, comic, experimental novel with a variety of puns, portmanteau words and the use of many languages. The events take place both in the real world and in a dream world. In the novel Mr and Mrs Porter live above a pub in Chapelizod in Dublin. They have three children: the twins, Kevin and Jerry, and a daughter, Issy. When the couple sleep, however, Mr Porter becomes Humphrey Chimpden Earwicker while Mrs Porter becomes Anna Livia Plurabelle; the twins become Shem and Shaun while Issy retains her name. There is hearsay about an indiscretion committed by Earwicker in the Phoenix Park – inappropriate behaviour with two young girls (perhaps voyeurism). Anna Livia defends her husband. The character Tim Finnegan, from the song of that name, is also introduced. He has 'died' after an accident on a construction site ('fell from a ladder and he broke his skull and they carried him home his corpse to wake'). The excerpt which follows is from the Anna Livia Plurabelle sequence, where two old women are washing clothes by the Liffey. When it is read aloud it is easier to understand.

From 'Anna Livia Plurabelle'

Well, you know or don't you kennet or haven't I told you every telling has a taling and that's the he and the she of it. Look, look, the dusk is growing! My branches lofty are taking root. And my cold cher's gone ashley. Fieluhr? Filou! What age is at? It saon is late. 'Tis endless now senne eye or erewone last saw Waterhouse's clogh. They took it asunder, I hurd thum sigh. When will they reassemble it? O, my back, my back, my bach! I'd want to go to Aches-les-Pains. Pingpong! There's the Belle for Sexaloitez! And Concepta de Send-us-pray! Pang! Wring out the clothes! Wring in the dew! Godavari, vert the showers! And grant thaya grace! Aman. Will we spread them here now? Ay, we will. Flip! Spread on your bank and I'll spread mine on mine. Flep! It's what I'm doing. Spread! It's churning chill. Der went is rising. I'll lay a few stones on the hostel sheets. A man and his bride embraced between them. Else I'd have sprinkled and folded them only. And I'll tie my butcher's apron here. It's suety yet. The strollers will pass it by. Six shifts, ten kerchiefs, nine to hold to the fire and this for the code, the convent napkins, twelve, one baby's shawl. Good mother Jossiph knows, she said. Whose head? Mutter snores? Deataceas! Wharnow are alle her childer, say? In kingdome gone or power to come or gloria be to them farther? Allalivial, allalluvial! Some here, more no more, more again lost alla stranger. I've heard tell that same brooch of the Shannons was married into a family in Spain. And all the Dunders de Dunnes in Markland's Vineland beyond Brendan's herring pool takes number nine in yangsee's hats. And one of Biddy's beads went bobbing till she rounded up lost histereve with a marigold and a cobbler's candle in a side strain of a main drain of a manzinahurries off Bachelor's Walk. But all that's left to the last of the Meaghers in the loup of the years prefixed and between is one kneebuckle and two hooks in the front. Do you tell me. that now? I do in troth. Orara por Orbe and poor Las Animas! Ussa, Ulla, we're umbas all! Mezha, didn't you hear it a deluge of times, ufer and ufer, respund to spond? You deed, you deed! I need, I need! It's that irrawaddyng I've stoke in my aars. It all but husheth the lethest zswound. Oronoko! What's your trouble? Is that the great Finnleader himself in his joakimono on his statue

riding the high horse there forehengist? Father of Otters, it is himself! Yonne there! Isset that? On Fallareen Common? You're thinking of Astley's Amphitheayter where the bobby restrained you making sugarstuck pouts to the ghostwhite horse of the Peppers. Throw the cobwebs from your eyes, woman, and spread your washing proper! It's well I know your sort of slop. Flap! Ireland sober is Ireland stiff Lord help you, Maria, full of grease, the load is with me! Your prayers. I sonht zo! Madammangut! Were you lifting your elbow, tell us, glazy cheeks, in Conway's Carrigacurra canteen? Was I what, hobbledyhips? Flop! Your rere gait's creakorheuman bitts your butts disagrees. Amn't I up since the damp dawn, marthared mary allacook, with Corrigan's pulse and varicoarse veins, my pramaxle smashed, Alice Jane in decline and my oneeyed mongrel twice run over, soaking and bleaching boiler rags, and sweating cold, a widow like me, for to deck my tennis champion son, the laundryman with the lavandier flannels? You won your limpopo limp fron the husky hussars when Collars and Cuffs was heir to the town and your slur gave the stink to Carlow. Holy Scamander, I sar it again! Near the golden falls. Icis on us! Seints of light! Zezere! Subdue your noise, you hamble creature! What is it but a blackburry growth or the dwyergray ass them four old codgers owns. Are you meanam Tarpey and Lyons and Gregory?

Chapelizod in the late nineteenth century. *Reproduced courtesy of the National Library of Ireland.*

Corner of Bachelor's Walk and O'Connell Bridge, 1897.
Reproduced courtesy of the National Library of Ireland.

I meyne now, thank all, the four of them, and the roar of them, that draves that stray in the mist and old Johnny MacDougal along with them. Is that the Poolbeg flasher beyant, pharphar, or a fireboat coasting nyar the Kishtna or a glow I behold within a hedge or my Garry come back from the Indes? Wait till the honeying of the lune, love! Die eve, little eve, die! We see that wonder in your eye. We'll meet again, we'll part once more. The spot I'll seek if the hour you'll find. My chart shines high where the blue milk's upset. Forgivemequick, I'm going! Bubye! And you, pluck your watch, forgetmenot. Your evenlode. So save to jurna's end! Mysights are swimming thicker on me by the shadows to this place. I sow home slowly now by own way, moy-valley way. Towy I too, rathmine.

Ah, but she was the queer old skeowsha anyhow, Anna Livia, trinkettoes! And sure he was the quare old buntz too, Dear Dirty Dumpling, foostherfather of fingalls and dotthergills. Gammer and gaffer we're all their gangsters. Hadn't he seven dams to wive him? And every dam had her seven crutches. And every crutch had its seven hues. And each hue had a differing cry. Sudds for me and supper for you and the doctor's bill for Joe John. Befor!

Bifur! He married his markets, cheap by foul, I know, like any Etrurian Catholic Heathen, in their pinky limony creamy birnies and their turkiss indienne mauves. But at milkidmass who was the spouse? Then all that was was fair. Tys Elvenland ! Teems of times and happy returns. The seim anew. Ordovico or viricordo. Anna was, Livia is, Plurabelle's to be. Northmen's thing made southfolk's place but howmulty plurators made eachone in person? Latin me that, my trinity scholard, out of eure sanscreed into oure eryan! Hircus Civis Eblanensis! He had buckgoat paps on him, soft ones for orphans. Ho, Lord! Twins of his bosom. Lord save us! And ho! Hey? What all men. Hot? His tittering daughters of. Whawk?

Can't hear with the waters of. The chittering waters of. Flittering bats, fieldmice bawk talk. Ho! Are you not gone ahome? What Thom Malone? Can't hear with bawk of bats, all thim liffeying waters of. Ho, talk save us! My foos won't moos. I feel as old as yonder elm. A tale told of Shaun or Shem? All Livia's daughtersons. Dark hawks hear us. Night! Night! My ho head halls. I feel as heavy as yonder stone. Tell me of John or Shaun? Who were Shem and Shaun the living sons or daughters of? Night now! Tell me, tell me, tell me, elm! Night night! Telmetale of stem or stone. Beside the rivering waters of, hitherandthithering waters of. Night!

Father and Son

After the death of his father, John Stanislaus Joyce, in December 1931, James Joyce felt a deep remorse, since he had not returned from Paris when the old man was dying. Following the birth of his grandson, Stephen James Joyce, in February 1932, Joyce wrote this poem in which he conflates the death of an old man with the birth of an infant. The title echoes the words of Pilate when he showed Christ to the crowd after he had been scourged: *Ecce homo* ('Behold the man'). *Ecce puer* means 'Behold the boy'. The play on life and death in the poem is a tour de force.

Ecce Puer

Of the dark past
A child is born.
With joy and grief
My heart is torn.

Calm in his cradle
The living lies.
May love and mercy
Unclose his eyes!

Young life is breathed
On the glass;
The world that was not
Comes to pass.

A child is sleeping:
An old man gone.
O, father forsaken,
Forgive your son!

CHAPTER 5

Dublinspeak

Irish regional accents are, in the main, quite easy to recognise – especially the southern Cork, Kerry and Limerick accents. In the north, the Belfast accent can usually be distinguished from the softer Derry and Donegal tones. The Dublin accent has traditionally been one of the easiest accents to distinguish, with its unique pronunciation and speech pattern. In recent times, however, this strongly accented 'Dublinspeak' has been declining, especially among younger people, whose accents have become more homogenised due to the influence of American culture.

Jovial cab driver by Harry Furniss, 1881.

Whether the way Dubliners speak is an accent or a dialect is a moot point. According to the late Professor Terry Dolan, former professor of English at University College Dublin, the two main influences on the way Dubliners speak are Elizabethan English and Hiberno-English, the former an echo of the dialect spoken by soldiers who were billeted in Dublin during the time of the Pale, the latter an attempt to translate directly from the Irish language, resulting in a unique speech pattern.

Moore Street market, 1962. *Reproduced courtesy of the National Library of Ireland.*

Echoes of Elizabethan English persist in the pronunciation of 'beat' as *bate*, 'tea' as *tay*, 'meat' as *mate*, 'more' as *mower*, 'roar' as *rower*, 'town' as *touwen* and so on. In the Irish language the word for the verb 'is' is *tá* (*thaw*). A *t* followed by a broad vowel in Irish will be pronounced *th*. When this structure is carried over into English there is a tendency to pronounce English words beginning with a *t* and followed by a broad vowel as *th* even when this is an incorrect pronunciation. Thus we regularly hear 'I thuck' for 'I took', and 'I thackled' for 'I tackled'.

By the same token, when *t* precedes a slender vowel in Irish it keeps this slender sound – for example, *tine* (meaning 'fire', pronounced *tinna*), *timpiste* (meaning 'accident', pronounced *timpishta*). So, when carried into the English language, words beginning with *th*, as in 'think', are often pronounced *tink*. A Dubliner might, therefore, pronounce 'I took my bag with me but I thought it was a little too heavy' as 'I thuck me bag with me bu'r I taught i' was a lihil thoo heavy'. The following sentence demonstrates the Dublin use of *me* for the possessive adjective *my* and the tendency to drop the last *t* in a verb ending in this consonant: 'Gerrouwa me way' ('Get out of my way').

Street vendor by Harry Furniss, 1881.

Some Dubliners regularly confuse the past tense with the past participle, especially with the verbs 'do' and 'see'. So we hear 'I seen the car' for 'I saw the car', and 'I done that job' for 'I did that job'. Past participles are often confused with the present participle as follows: 'I coulda killin' him' ('I could have killed him') and 'You coulda startin' a fire' ('You could have started a fire'). 'Our' can be pronounced 'er' which often results in misspelling among some Dubliners.

In standard English the second person singular is 'you', as is the second person plural. Centuries ago the second person singular was 'thou' and the second person plural was 'ye'. The Irish language uses *tú* for second person singular, but uses *sibh* for the second person plural. As Dublin people assimilated the English language they added an *s* to get the plural of 'you', coming up with 'yous'. This form of the second person plural can have a few versions, pronounced *youse, yez* or *yiz* – for example, 'Yiz are only a pack o' gurriers' ('You are only a pack of gurriers').

'Gameball' in Dublin speech expresses assent – for example, 'How are you getting on in your new job, Mick?' 'Gameball. I'm getting on grand.' The latter expression, 'grand', means that all is going well. A story is told that a wealthy Dublin man whose son had a very strong Dublin accent employed an Oxford professor, at great expense, to teach his son elocution. A few weeks later the Dublin man met the Oxford professor in O'Connell Street and asked, 'Well, how is my son doing at his elocution?' The professor replied, 'Gameball, gameball, bud, he's doin' grand!'

Dubliners regularly use redundant phrases for emphasis: 'He's a great little goer [fighter], he is' – the 'he is' being a redundant emphatic phrase. 'My sister is very good at maths, so she is' or 'I'll kill you dead, so I will!' are further examples.

In Dublinspeak the definite article is often substituted for the possessive adjective, so instead of saying 'my mother', a Dubliner will say 'the mother' (or 'the brother', 'the dad', 'the wife' and so on). A father will often be described as the old fellow ('the oul' fellah') while a mother may be described as the old one ('the oul' wan'). 'One' or *wan* can be used to describe a girl, as can 'fellow' or *fellah* to describe a boy – hence one hears 'young wans' and 'young fellahs'. Another Dublin word for a girl, girlfriend or wife is 'mot'.

There is a tendency in Dublin to use the suffix *o* when using a proper noun, so Declan will become *Deco*, Geraghty *Gerro* and Martin *Marto*. The same process is seen in place names, hence Montgomery Street (once a red light district) became the *Monto*. Even Christmas has been described as *Crimbo*! Dubliners also suffix *er* to words – for example, 'Look, he's on a reddener!' ('Look, he's blushing!'), 'Doyler' (Doyle), 'A little puddener' (a small plump child – from the noun 'pudding').

Many vulgar expletives can be heard in Dublin so it is not uncommon to hear an expletive inserted into a weekday, such as 'I'm goin' home Tues-fuckin-day' or 'at the week-fuckin-end!' or 'I'm not fuckin' goin'!'

One structure carried over from Irish into Hiberno-English is the present habitual tense. In standard English this would be used as follows: 'He is here every day at four'; but since in Irish there is a specific present habitual tense (*bím, bíonn tú, bíonn sé* and so on), Dubliners and other Irish people will often say 'He does be here every day at four' or 'I do come this way every Friday' ('I come this way every Friday').

In the Irish language there is no present perfect tense, so in order to say that one has just lost one's books, the idea is expressed as follows: *Tá mé tar éis mo leabhair a chailliúint* (literally: 'I'm after losing my books'). This results in 'I'm after', 'you're after', 'he's after' and so on being used when the present perfect would be used in standard English. Other examples are: 'Look, you're after spilling your drink' ('Look, you've spilt your drink') and 'We're after buying a new car' ('We've bought a new car').

The Irish expression *mo dhuine* (my man/person) to point out a specific man, or woman, has been carried over into Hiberno-English as 'your man' or 'your woman'. This is often pronounced *yer man* or *yer woman* and it is very common both in Dublin and beyond. 'Will yez look at the head on yer man!' 'Will yez look at the state of yer woman!'

English tourist at an Irish railway station by Georges du Maurier, 1881.

The digraph (two letters that express one sound) *th* is seldom pronounced correctly among Dubliners. Few go to the trouble of placing the tongue behind the front teeth to achieve this sound. Instead a *d* sound is used, so the demonstrative adjectives 'this', 'that', 'these' and 'those' are pronounced *dis, dat, dese* and *dose*. The definite article 'the' is pronounced *de*, as in 'De lesson was very long, it was'. When a word ends in a *t* sound it is often pronounced as a soft *t*: *rishe* (right), *cush* (cut).

Over the last few decades the strong Dublin accent, with its distinct pronunciation and grammatical idiosyncrasies has been declining, especially in the middle-class suburbs. A more homogenised accent has developed which is largely influenced by the American accent and vocabulary, as heard in American movies, media and television series. Young middle-class men and women will often pronounce 'about' as *abait*, 'crash' as *cresh*, 'party' as *pardy*, 'four' as *furr* and 'phone' as *foune* and so on. The superfluous 'like' may be heard in almost every sentence ('I was, like, at a lecture and it was, like, awesome') while upspeak, or the antipodean interrogative (making every sentence sound like a question), has also crept in. Today, even Irish newsreaders and broadcasters do not hesitate to use such American corporate terms as 'ramp up' (intensify), 'kick off' (start), 'conversation' (discussion), 'going forward' (in future), 'window' (opportunity), 'flag' (indicate) and 'roll out' (introduce), while 'I'm good' is replacing 'I'm well', and 'cheers' is replacing 'thanks'.

This manner of speaking has now reduced many regional accents in Ireland to a common homogenised base. Sociologists have suggested that the accent is an attempt, on the part of younger people, to associate with an 'upwardly mobile' class. The accent in question has been captured by the author Paul Howard in his Ross O'Carroll Kelly novels – an excerpt from one of which is included later in this book. The popularity of such middle-class accents can result in young people who speak with flat inner-city Dublin accents being discriminated against and marginalised.

The issue of whether Dublinspeak is simply an acceptable form of dialect or an incorrect use of grammar and syntax is open to debate. It will be interesting to see how the English language in Dublin, and beyond, evolves over the coming years.

CHAPTER 6

Dublin Street Games

In the late Pete St John's popular ballad 'Dublin in the Rare Ould Times', he mentions 'the haunting children's rhymes'. Such rhymes are part and parcel of street games that stretch back through the ages, reflecting a time when Dublin children spent many of their days on the street – especially during the summer season. Some of their games still survive today, often with different names, as in 'hopscotch' replacing 'beds', but the cultural bedrock of Dublin street games will always be an important talking point from generation to generation.

Nowadays in Dublin (and elsewhere) children are less likely to play street games for several reasons. Many parents are reluctant to allow their children out for fear of traffic accidents, assault or even abduction. With modern technology, children are more likely to be involved in more sedentary activities such as playing computer games or engaging with social media on their smartphones and tablets. Over fifty years ago, however, Dublin children engaged in a variety of street games and rhymes, especially on long summer days and evenings. The following are some of the more memorable street games played on Dublin's streets during my childhood in the 1950s and 1960s.

Ballymun, 1969.
Reproduced courtesy of the National Library of Ireland.

Skipping

In the past, skipping was generally considered a 'girl's game' and there were two types: one involved a single girl skipping alone with a skipping rope; the other involved two girls swinging a longer rope while other girls skipped in and out skilfully. Sometimes as many as eight girls were skipping at the one time. What made the game memorable, however, were the songs that the girls sang in rhythm to the skipping:

> Cinderella dressed in yella,
> Went downstairs to kiss a fella,
> Made a mistake and kissed a snake,
> How many doctors did it take?
> One, two, three ...

and

> Vote vote vote for De Valera
> Here comes Debbie at the door,
> Debbie is the one who will have a bit of fun
> And we won't need Mary any more.

and

See see my playmate
Come and play with me
My dolly has the flu
And the German measles too
Fly over the rainbow
Into my alley-o
Forever more
One, two, three, four ...

The speed of the rope being swung could vary: slow, medium or fast. The fast speed was called a 'pepper'. The height at which the rope was swung could also vary from low (brushing the ground) to high (a foot off the ground). If a girl skipped to a high 'pepper', she had to be very agile indeed. More often than not, the rope would eventually get caught up in her legs and she was then 'out'. Being out in this case was called 'missaloopio'.

Beds (or Hopscotch)

There were two forms of the game 'beds'. The first involved chalking a series of numbered boxes with three transepts onto the path. A small shoe-polish tin, weighted with clay (called a 'piggy'), was then thrown into one of the boxes. The girl or boy hopped on one foot through the numbered boxes and picked up the 'piggy' until they lost their balance or put their foot over one of the chalked lines. Then it was the next child's turn. The boy or girl who lasted the longest without losing balance or crossing the chalked lines was the winner.

Girls often played a more challenging form of the game: a numbered rectangle was chalked on the path and the contestants had to kick the 'piggy' gently with one foot into the boxes. Boys seldom played this form of the game, as they were generally not as skilful at it.

The following poem, from my collection *Common Ground* (1996), uses the game of 'beds' metaphorically to describe the battle of the sexes.

Beds

The polish tin *piggy* weighted with clay,
is tossed, with elliptical
precision, into the chalked beds –
Girls, in summer dresses,
hop, skip and turn, their
pigtails undulating on the air –

Here is grace in movement,
the negotiation of white-sandalled feet
and scudding tin, the elegant patience
of waiting in line, the piping final tally
before the game begins again.

Excluded from their beds for lack of
grace
we observe from the sideline, catcalling
enviously,
disturbed by gracious pirouette
and billowing dresses.

Beds by Fred Conlon.

In desperation, we will paint on the veneer
of manners, cultivating
wit and charm, the ground rules
of an ageless game, returning,
with pseudo-grace, to observe,
once more, from the sideline,
to negotiate insidiously, to inveigle our way
at last, into their beds.

Street Football

In street football, the 'goalposts' were created by placing jumpers or jackets on the street or road. In the game called 'three and in', if a boy scored three times, he became the goalkeeper. While few wanted to be goalkeeper, all made a great effort nonetheless to score! Since playing football on the road was prohibited, if a garda approached on his bicycle the ball was hidden away and the jumpers snapped up, while the boys disappeared as quickly as possible from sight.

Other games of street football involved more standard football rules but with four or five players per team. It was a mark of esteem to be the first chosen by a designated captain and a very humbling experience to be last chosen, generally because such a boy was perceived to have 'two left feet'. To my shame, I was always among such boys when a captain chose his team!

Broken Statues

In this game, one child was nominated as 'it' and the other boys and girls stood or sat on a low wall or railing. When 'it' gave the signal, one boy or girl jumped down and immediately froze in whatever position they landed. 'It' then made funny faces or gestures – the object being to make the boy or girl laugh and move from their frozen position. This continued until all had been counted out by laughing or moving.

The following poem, published in my collection *Common Ground* (1996), recalls the above game but, on a metaphoric level, it promotes iconoclasm.

Shattered Icons

When you jumped from
the railings, you stood
transfixed, frozen in time,
holding your ludicrous positions,
until simian grimaces
cracked even the most rigid
among your infant ranks –
There among the broken statues,
you laugh at shattered form
until the tears stream
down your impish faces.

The frozen smiles of politicians
commend the power of icons

on pedestals of Church and State –
and I search for cracks again,
with iconoclastic zeal,
to shatter rigid form,
to laugh at broken statues.

Conkers (or Chestnuts)

Conkers was predominantly a boy's game when I was young, played in autumn when chestnuts were plentiful. A string was strung through a hole bored in the chestnut and knotted so the nut could then be used in contest. One boy held the chestnut steady on its string while the other struck it with his own chestnut or 'conker'. Eventually one chestnut was smashed and the intact one was declared the winner. This then became 'conker number one' until it was defeated, and so on. The most successful strategy here was to place a chestnut in the chimney flue and leave it there for months. As it dried out it became rock-hard and was called a 'seasoner' or a 'hacker'. James Joyce refers to such a chestnut in his novel *A Portrait of the Artist as a Young Man*: 'It was Wells who had shouldered him into the square ditch because he would not swop his little snuffbox for Wells's seasoned hacking chestnut, the conqueror of forty.'

A horse chestnut with a hole bored ready to be threaded onto a string for a game of conkers.

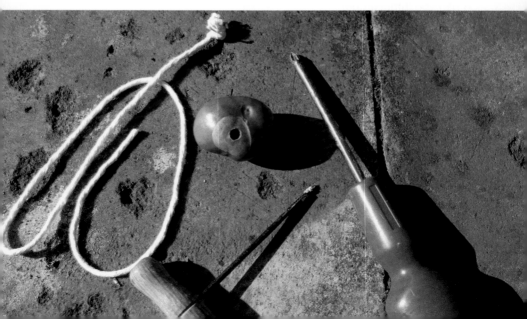

In the following poem, from my collection *Common Ground*, I recall my own childhood experience of this game in the Dublin suburbs. The lines become figurative, however, as they describe the creative process where the broad leaves of the horse chestnut tree become the discarded pages (leaves) of the writer as he or she tries, repeatedly, to strive after perfection.

Conkers

We flung sticks repeatedly into the chestnut trees
around the Glebe House, until the thorny capsules
tumbled to earth in a damburst of leaves –

Our feet crushed the husks, our nails exposed the
    gleaming
chestnuts, each half-moon redolent of autumn,
as we strung them on knotted cords, ready for battle.

From Crumlin Cross to Windmill Lane,
we duelled with swingeing blows,
splitting and shattering, notching our scores –

A seasoned hacker, flue-dried for a year, could
    devastate
the largest conker, could shatter with tempered
    resilience,
its gnarled form enduring long out of season.

My crumpled leaves speak the wisdom
of seasonable temper, of chestnuts taken from the
    fire,
of bright half-moons rising from the husk:
I write to conquer.

CHAPTER 7

Dublin Characters

One of the most striking features of Dublin City down through the years has been the variety of its characters. These have ranged from street poets and balladeers to more recent characters such as the Diceman and Dancing Mary. Their colour and eccentricity have marked them out and each has been affectionately remembered by the Dublin public to such an extent that nightclubs and pubs now bear their names.

The Grangegorman Lane Murder and William Davis (Billy in the Bowl)

In late-eighteenth-century Dublin, many beggars survived on the charity of the 'big houses' and that of the public in general. One such beggar was William Davis, better known as 'Billy in the Bowl'. Davis had been born without legs yet he made his way round the streets of Stoneybatter, Dublin, in a large cast-iron bowl on wheels, which had been fashioned for him by a local blacksmith. He propelled himself along using his powerful, muscular arms. Davis was a very handsome young man with thick black hair, dark eyes and an aquiline nose, so he easily charmed the servant girls from the big houses in Oxmantown. Moved by the plight of such a handsome disabled man begging, they would give him pennies and even scraps of food from their houses.

Stoneybatter, 2022.

Davis did well on his pickings, but he developed a gambling habit and became a heavy drinker, so his meagre money was soon spent. In order to replenish this, he devised a devious strategy to rob unsuspecting female victims: putting his bowl aside, he hid in the bushes along Stoneybatter, which was then a country road. He screamed out 'in pain', and when a passing servant girl came to investigate, he grasped her with his powerful arms so tightly that she passed out. He then snatched her purse. When the unfortunate servant girl came to, she was unable to describe her attacker, so Davis went on robbing women while no one suspected the poor crippled beggar.

Soon after, he attacked another servant girl but this time it did not go to plan, as she was a strong country girl and she put up a stout resistance. Davis panicked and was forced to strangle her. Her murder, known as the Grangegorman Lane murder, caused a stir, and since Dublin's first police force had recently been mobilised, in 1786, it became their first case. Davis was forced to lie low for a while, but he soon reverted to his old ways and attacked a cook on her way home from work.

This young lady was not alone, however. Davis had not noticed that her friend was by her side. The two women fought back fiercely. One grabbed Davis by the hair while the other took a pin from her hat and poked him in the eye. The beggar's screams alerted the public and he was conveyed to Green Street Prison on a wheelbarrow after the women's valuables had been recovered.

Since the murder of the servant girl could not be proven in law, Davis was jailed for robbery and assault. While in Green Street Prison, many people came to visit him, out of curiosity, while he did hard labour with his strong arms. Given that there were no more robberies in the area it was assumed that Davis had indeed been the perpetrator of the Grangegorman Lane murder.

Jack Scott, 1st Earl of Clonmel (Copperfaced Jack)

Jack Scott aka Copperfaced Jack (1739–98) was born in Tipperary to an aristocratic family. Having attended Kilkenny College, he studied law at Trinity College and the Middle Temple in London. Called to the bar in 1765, four years later he became a member of parliament for Mullingar until 1773. Scott went on to hold such distinguished positions as privy councillor and attorney general for Ireland and Lord Chief Justice.

John Scott by Gilbert Stuart.

By 1784 he had also been created 1st Baron Earlsfort of Lisson-Earl, County Tipperary. So given to snuff, overeating and drinking, Baron Earlsfort became grossly overweight and his ruddy complexion explained his nickname, 'Copperfaced Jack'. He reputedly made many resolutions to live more moderately, but he rarely succeeded.

Scott was a rude, arrogant man who made many enemies accordingly. The writer Frank Hopkins, in his book *Hidden Dublin*, describes how the baron had a Dublin journalist, John Magee, jailed on a libel charge.

After Magee's release he bought a plot of land adjacent to Scott's house near Seapoint, County Dublin. There he organised 'days of great amusement' every weekend. After such drunken sports as sack races, dancing dogs and pole-climbing, Magee released several pigs, which ran through Scott's beautiful gardens destroying the flower beds and shrubs.

Scott died at the age of fifty-eight in 1798. He is reputed to have said that for all he achieved in life he would rather have his youth again – as a young chimney-sweep.

While in Dublin, Scott lived in Harcourt Street, and today one of Dublin's most popular nightclubs on that street is named after him. Frequented by a clientele of nurses, gardaí and GAA players – not to mention celebrities – the nightclub is famous for 'the shift'[1] and even has a wall nicknamed 'the shifting wall'.

A musical entitled *Copper Face Jacks: The Musical* by Paul Howard has been running in Dublin theatres since 2018. Perhaps Jack Scott would turn in his grave but, on the other hand, since he was a man given to excess himself, perhaps he would be proud!

The Strange Story of the Dolocher

In the late eighteenth century a debtor's prison stood in the area of Dublin now known as Cornmarket. Here debtors were imprisoned until their debts were repaid, but the prison also housed other prisoners who had to pay for the luxury of a flea-ridden bed. This prison was known as Black Dog Prison after a tavern of that name nearby.

One prisoner, who was called Olocher, had been tried for the murder and rape of a local woman. He cheated the gallows at Gallows Green (in present-day Baggot Street) by committing suicide in his cell.

Soon after his death a sentry on duty near Cork Street was attacked and rendered unconscious at his post. When he recovered sufficiently, he told how he

[1] Slang for French kissing.

had been attacked by a horrible creature, half man and half black pig. This creature was seen by other guards on sentry duty and hysteria gripped the city, with many soldiers too terrified to man their sentry posts.

One guard from Black Dog Prison, however, dismissed the story of the creature and was happy to go on guard duty, but the following morning, his colleagues found, to their horror, that he had vanished, leaving only his uniform and rifle. People were convinced that the infernal creature had devoured this poor man and that the unholy spirit of Olocher had come back as a demon to continue his evil ways. This belief was substantiated when a number of women were attacked by the creature.

Last remaining gatehouse of the original Dublin City wall, 1240, leading to St Audoen's Church, Cornmarket.

There was consternation in inner city Dublin, with people remaining in their homes after nightfall in mortal terror of what they now called 'the Dolocher'. The matter was taken so seriously that a group of men decided to kill every pig they found on the streets. During this time these animals were very plentiful, as many families kept pigs. A huge cull took place but, mysteriously, not a single dead animal was found on the street the following day.

Then, one wet evening, a local blacksmith left a tavern in the inner city. He was clad in a woman's cloak and bonnet given to him by the barmaid, since the downpour was especially heavy. Hearing a snarling behind him, he turned and faced the Dolocher. The blacksmith was strong and healthy, however, and aided by other men who rushed out from the local taverns, he made short work of his attacker. On the ground, mortally injured, lay a man dressed in the skin and head of a black pig.

The man proved to be the missing sentry from Black Dog Prison, who admitted to spreading stories of the Dolocher before dressing up in the black pig's skin and head in order to rob terrified women. He had also got rid of the carcasses of the pigs after the cull. The man died from injuries inflicted after he had been beaten by the crowd and so ended the story of the Dolocher, which is still told in Dublin centuries later.

Zozimus

Michael J. Moran, aka Zozimus, was called 'the last of the gleemen'. A gleeman was a wandering minstrel or poet common in medieval Europe. The gleeman was on a lower social scale to jesters and jugglers, who were often employed full-time by kings and aristocrats.

Zozimus, the blind bard.

Moran took his nickname from that of Zozimus of Palestine, a fifth-century ascetic and saint who is reputed to have converted Mary of Egypt. She had gone to the Holy Land, initially, with the intention of seducing pilgrims, but was persuaded to renounce the flesh by Zozimus. A long poem entitled 'Mary of Egypt', composed by the Bishop of Raphoe, was often requested and quoted by Moran. In time, he adopted the name Zozimus.

Moran was born in Faddle Alley in the Liberties of Dublin in 1794. He became blind due to illness when he was an infant. As a wandering rhymer he developed an exceptional memory and could quote verse at will. His poems, most of which he composed himself, covered religious themes, politics and current events. Zozimus cut a strange figure in his long scalloped coat, greasy old beaver hat and heavy brogues. He carried a blackthorn stick, which was attached to his wrist so that he could swing it freely.

He plied his trade from Wood Quay to Grafton Street urging his audience to listen intently, as follows:

Ye sons and daughters of Erin,
Gather round poor Zozimus, yer friend,
Listen boys until yiz hear
Me charming song so dear.

Moran had many brushes with the Dublin Metropolitan Police, who frowned on ballad singers and street performers, but the public loved him, and they marvelled at his capacity to memorise and to quote with real conviction.

He died in 1846 at his home in Patrick Street and was buried in Glasnevin in an unmarked grave. He specifically asked to be buried in Glasnevin, as there were look-out posts around its walls which discouraged body snatchers from stealing recently buried corpses for dissection. In the late 1960s the Dublin City Ramblers ballad group and the Smith Brothers of the Submarine Bar in Crumlin raised a headstone over his grave, which reads:

Zozimus
To the memory
Of
Michael Moran
Poet
Street Singer
Born 1794
Died 1846
R.I.P.

Sing a song for oul Zozimus
As always from the heart
Your name will forever live
As a Dubliner apart.

In more recent years, Inchicore poet and historian Liam O'Meara has written extensively about Moran's life and work in a book entitled *Zozimus: Life and Works of Michael Moran*.

One famous ballad attributed to Zozimus is 'The Twangman'. This tells the story of the revenge exacted on a commercial traveller who stole the Twangman's mot ('girl' in Dublin slang).

The Twangman

Come listen to my story
'Tis about a nice young man
When the Militia wasn't wantin'
He dealt in hawkin' twang
He loved a lovely maiden
As fair as any midge
An' she kept a traycle depot
Wan side of the Carlisle bridge.[2]

2   This is now O'Connell Bridge.

Another man came a courtin' her
And his name was Mickey Baggs
He was a commercial traveller
An' he dealt in bones and rags
Well he took her out to Sandymount
For to see the waters rowl
An' he stole the heart of the Twangman's girl
Playin' 'Billy-in-the-bowl'

Oh, when the Twangman heard of this
He flew into a terrible rage
And he swore be the contents of his twang cart
On him he'd have revenge
So he stood in wait near James's Gate
Till the poor old Baggs came up
With his twang knife, sure he took the life
Of the poor ould gather 'em up.

And it's now yis have heard my story
And I hope yis'll be good men
And not go chasing the Twangman's mot
Or any other oul' hen
For she'll leave you without a brass farthing
Not even your ould sack of rags
And that's the end of the story
Of poor old Mickey Baggs.

Bang Bang

Bang Bang (left), c.1966.

One of Dublin's most famous characters, Thomas Dudley, aka Bang Bang, was born in the inner city in 1906 to John and Mary Dudley of Clarence Street. John Dudley was a chimney-sweep. After his parents' early deaths, Thomas was brought up in an orphanage in Cabra. As an adult, he lived in Mill Street in the Coombe.

Between the 1920s and the late 1960s he travelled regularly on both trams and buses carrying a large silver key in his hand, which he used as a 'revolver'. Obsessed with cowboy films, Dudley would point the key at the conductor or the passengers, shouting 'Bang, bang' – hence his nickname. Since he was seen as a harmless eccentric, the Dublin public would participate in the cowboy fantasy by 'shooting' back at him or pretending to fall down dead.

As he would often interrupt films and plays by 'shooting' at the actors, he was barred from most city centre cinemas. On one occasion he fell off a bus in O'Connell Street. When the driver stopped the bus and the worried passengers alighted to check on his condition, he jumped up from the ground laughing and saying, 'Carry on, I'm only wounded!'

As he grew older his sight failed and he was cared for by the Rosminian Fathers in Drumcondra. After he died there in 1981, the blind patients in care in the centre filed past his coffin and poignantly touched his features. He was buried in an unmarked grave in St Joseph's Cemetery, Drumcondra, but thirty-six years later a plaque was erected over his grave after a fundraising campaign by Daniel Lambert, owner of the Bang Bang café in Phibsborough. A large key resembling his original 'revolver' decorates the plaque. The original key can now be seen in the reading room of the Dublin City Archive in Pearse Street.

I wrote the following poem, from my collection *Fearful Symmetry* (1990), to commemorate Bang Bang and I referred to other 'urban cowboys', as depicted in Flann O'Brien's famous novel *At Swim-Two-Birds*.

Urban Cowboys 1966

Cher's haunting song rings in our ears
as we start to his report –
riding shotgun on the buses
he fires at point blank range,
even as we raise our hands
in mock surrender.

From the Barn to the Ranch,[3]
from the Flatlands of Rathmines
to the Badlands of Crumlin and Kimmage,
no desperado has blazed so crazy a trail
since Shorty Andrews and Slug Willard
rode out from Ringsend.

As large as Tie me Up, Fortycoats
or Billy in the Bowl, he holds the key
to the city, the oddest six shooter
in Dublin history

3   The Barn is short for Dolphin's Barn in Dublin; the Ranch is a housing estate in Inchicore near the Inchicore Works.

'Bang Bang,' that awful sound,[4]
'Bang Bang,' we hit the ground,
'Bang Bang,' Tom Dudley shot us down.

4   From the singer
Cher's 1966 song
'Bang Bang'.

Johnny Fortycoats

Johnny Fortycoats, whose real name was P.J. Marlow, was a familiar figure on the streets of Dublin in the 1930s and '40s. While he did not wear forty coats, he did wear at least four or five coats regardless of the weather. He often begged outside churches on Sundays and admitted that he did well financially on these occasions. Marlow was a very popular character and was well-loved – especially by Dublin children, who would shout after him, 'Fortycoats, Fortycoats, how many coats are you wearing today?' He would then chase them playfully. His habit of spitting on the floor meant that he was barred from many restaurants.

Johnny Fortycoats, 1943. *Reproduced courtesy of the National Library of Ireland.*

Children often walked about with him because, in the pockets of his many coats, he kept comics and sweets. There was some confusion about the precise date of his death because many Dublin vagrants looked like Fortycoats, but Marlow is believed to have died in the mid-1940s. The actor Fran Dempsey played the character of Fortycoats in a popular Irish television series for children in the 1980s.

The Ragmen

Ragmen collected unwanted household items, including old clothes, to sell on to merchants. Long ago the ragman plied his trade on foot, carrying a small bag flung over his shoulder. In this was the scavenged material, often containing bones and metal, hence the term 'rag and bone man'. I can still recall such ragmen who traded cheap toys for old clothes. They travelled by horse and cart and rang a bell to attract the attention of local children, who rushed out of their houses with a selection of old rags.

This poem, from my collection *Common Ground*, recalls my own childhood memories of the ragmen and their subsequent demise as children's interests became more technologically defined and their toys much more sophisticated.

A horse and cart on a
Dublin street, 2006.

Ragman
The tolling bell and raucous voice
ranging over gardens, sent children
scurrying like wood lice, to return
and convert rags to riches
upon his mystery cart,
while his piebald mare,
smelling of jaded leather
jingled her harness and stamped
restlessly in the straddle.

He bartered gaudy toys, garish
windmills, coloured birds on strings,
whistles and balloons –
An old coat launched a glider
in looping flight, six jam jars
armed a warrior with crude tin weapons.

The bell tolls for his travelling clan,
in Hiace vans on grim hard shoulders
running the gauntlet of stones –
While tablets and gaudy soaps
hold restless children in the straddle
of confinement, I tilt at garish windmills
to write the ragman's requiem.

The Dublin ballad below was sung originally by Ronnie Drew of the Dubliners on an album in 1964. The hilarious events described in the song took place in Ash Street in the Liberties of Dublin, near the Coombe. According to a radio documentary produced in 1982 by the late David Warner, the song was collected by Colm O'Lochlainn in 1913 from a ballad singer. It appears in O'Lochlainn's *Irish Street Ballads*. In this documentary, elderly residents of Ash Street and the Coombe were interviewed. They could actually identify some of the characters in the song, such as Kieran Grace, Humpy Soodelum and Liza Boland. The original ballad was longer than the Dubliners' version, and the ragmen eventually settled down to eat fish and chips from an Italian chip shop on Thomas Street rather than 'some ham parings'!

The Night of the Ragman's Ball

Come listen to me for a while
Me good friends one and all
And I'll sing to you a verse or two
About a famous ball
Now the ball was given be some friends
Who lived down in Ash Street
In a certain house in the Liberties
Where the ragmen used to meet

Well the names were called at seven o'clock
And every man was on the spot
And to show respect for the management
Every ragman brought his mot
I must admit that I brought mine
At twenty-five minutes to eight
And the first to stand up was Kieran Grace
For to tell me I was late.

Then up jumps Humpy Soodelum
And he says: 'I think somehow
By the ways yiz are goin' on tonight
Yiz are a looking for a row.
Now listen here, Grace, if you want your face
You'd better not shout or bawl
There's a lot of hard chaws gonna be here tonight
To respect the ragman's ball.'

Then says my one, 'You're a quare one now
And Biddy you're hard to beat,'
Oh when up jumps Liza Boland
And she told her to hold her prate
Then my one made a clout at her
She missed her and hit the wall
And the two of them went in the ambulance
The night of the Ragman's ball

Well for eating we had plenty now
As much as we could hold
We drank Brady's Loopline porter
Until round the floor we rolled
In the midst of all the confusion
Someone shouted for a song
When up jumps oul' John Lavin and sings
'Keep rollin' your barrel along'

Then we all sat down to some ham parings
When everything was quiet
And for broken noses I must say
We had a lovely night
Black eyes they were in great demand
Not to mention split heads and all
So if anyone wants to commit suicide
Let him come to the Ragman's ball.

Thom McGinty aka the Diceman (1952–95)

During the '80s and '90s Grafton Street in Dublin
boasted a variety of street performers. These ranged
from classical and traditional musicians to Charlie
Chaplin lookalikes and jugglers. By far the most
colourful of these artists, however, was Thom McGinty
aka the Diceman. Born in Glasgow in 1952 to Irish
parents, Thom had come to Ireland in 1976 to pose
naked for art students at the National College of Art
and Design and had fallen in love with the city.

He advertised for the Diceman games shop, having
begun his street career as a clown in the Dandelion

Market – originally on the site of the present-day Stephen's Green Centre. Adopting the title of the games shop as his 'stage name', the Diceman McGinty appeared in a variety of costumes on Grafton Street, where he achieved legendary status by standing stock still until a coin was placed at his feet, upon which he would wink dramatically and smile. When moved on by the gardaí, he would walk, in slow motion, to the spontaneous applause of the onlookers.

Standing stock still was a hard task given that some members of the public liked to pinch him or walk on his feet when he stood barefoot, while others dropped lit cigarettes in his path when he was walking in slow motion. McGinty carried on despite such distractions and was much loved by the Dublin public.

The Diceman travelled widely to take part in many street festivals abroad, from Paris to Moscow. He took part in the Gate Theatre production of Oscar Wilde's *Salome*, standing perfectly still and then executing John the Baptist – in slow motion. He advertised for the film *Mona Lisa*, directed by Neil Jordan, appearing in a wig and holding a picture frame around his face to create a comic impression of the famous Da Vinci

The Diceman.
Reproduced courtesy of the National Library of Ireland.

painting. He lived near Spiddal in Galway and would take the train to Dublin.

He was twice interviewed by the broadcaster Gay Byrne on the *Late Late Show*. In the second interview, in 1990, McGinty confirmed that he had tested positive for HIV. The Diceman died in 1995 at the age of forty-two, and his coffin was carried down Grafton Street to the sustained applause of the onlookers.

The Diceman has been celebrated in poems by Paula Meehan and Liam O'Meara, while a moving tribute to the artist was made by the late poet Brendan Kennelly. Plaques commemorating him can be seen in Tralee and Baltinglass. The actor Alan Stanford has regularly proposed a statue of the performer but, to date, this has not been commissioned.

Mary Dunne aka Dancing Mary (1927–2014)

During the 1980s when the Anna Livia fountain was at the top of O'Connell Street, Mary Dunne could be seen there almost daily. She was a very religious woman and, besides dancing, tried to interest the passers-by in the Legion of Mary as well as handing out religious magazines and holy pictures. She wore large rosary beads around her neck and was always dressed impeccably. Even after the fountain was removed, Mary continued to frequent the same spot, originally singing and later, when her voice failed, dancing unselfconsciously and twirling about. She claimed that she danced to honour the Virgin Mary and the Holy Trinity.

She was known as 'Mad Mary' or, more sensitively, 'Dancing Mary'. She kept her pockets full of Milky Mints sweets and would often share these with children who went by. As the years passed her eyesight failed but she continued to dance until 2002, when her health failed.

In 2010 Eamonn Campbell of the Dubliners organised a street concert in her honour, which was the measure of her fame. Originally from Kilkenny, she is believed to have worked as a hairdresser in Dublin and during the '60s lived with her husband and six children in Geneva.

Dubliners were amused by her, and they knew she was a harmless eccentric. She gained Facebook notoriety on a tribute page entitled 'Who remembers the woman that danced on O'Connell St beside the Anna Livia', which boasted over 24,000 likes. Her son would collect her from the city centre every evening at about 3.30 and bring her home to her house in Dún Laoghaire. The Facebook interest prompted many newspapers to publish articles on her.

When Mary passed away in 2014, her funeral Mass took place in the Church of the Holy Family in Dún Laoghaire, and she was buried in Deans Grange Cemetery. The many tributes that flooded in spoke to her popularity as a well-loved Dublin character.

The Anna Livia
Plurabelle monument,
O'Connell Street, 1989.

CHAPTER 8

From the Boards to the Silver Screen

While theatre in Dublin dates back to Norman times, the Werburgh Street Theatre, built circa 1637, appears to be the first custom-built theatre in the capital. It was associated with the famous English dramatist James Shirley, but it had a very short life – it closed during the rebellion of 1641. Twenty years later, after the restoration of the English monarchy in Ireland, Smock Alley Theatre (originally named the Theatre Royal) was established in Dublin by John Ogilby. Here pro-Stuart and Shakespearean classics were staged. The Queen's Theatre and the Gaiety Theatre both opened in Dublin in the nineteenth century and staged popular melodramas. It was not until the establishment of the Irish Literary Theatre in 1889 and the Abbey Theatre in 1904 that Dublin audiences saw plays written by Irish playwrights that dealt with real Irish themes.

The first dedicated cinema in Dublin was the Volta, which opened in 1909. This cinema is perhaps most famous because it was managed by James Joyce for a short time. As cinema burgeoned after the silent films of the 1920s had been replaced by 'talkies', Dublin City saw the proliferation of such cinemas as the Carlton, the Metropole, the Royal and so on. By 1956 there were no fewer than fifty-six cinemas in

The Abbey Theatre by Liam C. Martin, 1960. *Reproduced courtesy of the National Library of Ireland.*

the county of Dublin. As television replaced cinema-going, however, by the 1980s only the larger cinemas managed to survive, and many of these today are state of the art, with ten screens or more.

The Abbey Theatre

The Abbey Theatre, or National Theatre of Ireland, was founded by Lady Gregory, Edward Martyn and W.B. Yeats in 1899. When a building became available in Lower Abbey Street, it was fitted out as a theatre and opened in December 1904. Here, Máire Nic Shiúbhlaigh (Mary Walker), one of the first Abbey actors, describes the opening night. This extract is interesting, as it mentions poet W.B. Yeats and playwrights Lady Augusta Gregory and John Millington Synge, as well as actors and theatre-founders Frank and Willie Fay.

First Night at the Abbey

The theatre opened for the first time on a Tuesday, 27 December 1904. It is easy to describe. ... As was only to be expected on such an occasion, we had a full house. ... Yeats was impressive in evening dress, and kept coming behind the scenes to see how things were getting along.

Back stage, Willie Fay, dressed for his part in one of the new plays, a wild wig slipping sideways over his elfin face, swung unexpectedly from a batten high in the flys, arranging the lighting.

Standing as far out of the way as possible, those of us who were unoccupied, ate a scrap meal of bread and cocoa. It was all we had had to eat for hours. Every member of the society had been in the theatre since early afternoon. In between bites we watched the auditorium through a crack in the curtain. The pit and gallery were full. The stalls were slower in filling, but the crowd was increasing all the time. A number of people sitting in front seemed oblivious of the pre-curtain chatter as they listened to the violin music of Arthur Darley, our one musician.

Darley was a great addition to the little-known company. A violinist of note, he was a well-known collector of traditional Irish airs. Yeats had taken him along to play between the acts when we were in Molesworth Hall.

The sound of a familiar voice drew our attention back-stage again. In a dark corner, sitting on an upturned property-basket, sat Synge himself, rolling the inevitable cigarettes.

'God bless you,' he said. 'I hope that you're as happy as I am. I am so honoured that my little play should be chosen for the first week.' *In the Shadow of the Glen* was billed for the second night.

For our opening we played a triple bill: Yeats's new one-act *On Baile's Strand*; a revival of *Kathleen Ni Houlihan*; and gave the first production of *Spreading the News*, Lady Gregory's clever little cameo of an Irish fair-day incident. During the following week Synge's play was shuffled with Lady Gregory's in support of *On Baile's Strand*.

Poster for the Abbey
Theatre, March 1908.
*Reproduced courtesy of
the National Library of
Ireland.*

Many considered that Yeats's new play was his best. In it, as one writer put it, he emerged from the shadows with less of the mystic and more of the human element in the composition than in some of his earlier verse plays. The piece, a dramatic setting of the legend telling of the slaying of his own son by the unwitting Cuchulainn, belonged to an older order of drama than some of his other lyrical works. With the introduction of Barach, the fool, Yeats approached the Shakespearian model, but never sacrificed the originality of treatment, wrote the reviewers. ...

The evening progressed. In the auditorium, the audience, filling every seat, lining the walls of the balcony and pit, watched eagerly, a sea of faces stirring with enthusiasm. The subtle humour of Lady Gregory's new play, the first of her famous 'Cloon' comedies, captured the heart of all. The overbearing 'Removable Magistrate' and his dull-witted policeman, Jo Muldoon, seeking out the perpetrator of a crime that was never committed; the melancholy Bartley Fallon, hand-cuffed to the infuriated Jack Smith, whom he is supposed to have killed; his mournful fear that if they are put together in a cell, 'murder will be done that time surely' – a perfect piece of dignified comedy by Willie Fay.

And then the scene had changed. The curtain had risen on the new Yeats play. I was standing in the wings, a forgotten prompt script in my hand. Willie Fay, the comedian, the business-like stage-manager of a few moments before was no more. He was transformed into a tiny ragged sprite, cringing before the glittering king of his brother. The other figures paled into the background. Frank Fay spoke, fondling his lines, and they flowed out across the footlights, hovering a moment over the hushed auditorium, his little figure gaining power through the beauty of his words; first as the proud king, hero of a thousand battles, then as the horrified, grief-stricken father, verging on madness, his anguish intensified by the quiet irony of the fool. That moment – a brief one in a memorable evening – will remain long in my memory. The Fays had never acted so well together.

That evening ended too soon. Silently we gathered on the darkened stage, the muffled roar of the applause coming through the fallen curtain. Yeats passed through the green-room door, crossed the set, then stepped in front of the audience. Faintly the words came back: 'We shall take as our mottos those words written over the three gates of the City of Love of Edmund Spenser – over the first gate was "Be bold!"; over the second "Be bold, be bold! And evermore be bold!"; and over the third, "Yet be not too bold" ...'

More applause. The tiny building vibrating with the echoes. Then quiet, and the murmur of voices as the audience began to file out. Back-stage, I remember, Frank Fay spoke first. He said: 'This is only the beginning ...'

The Volta – Dublin's First Dedicated Cinema

On 20 December 1909 at 45 Mary Street, Dublin, the Volta Cinema, initially known as the Cinematograph Volta, opened its doors to the public. While films had been shown before that on an ad hoc basis, it was the first dedicated cinema in the city.

The twenty-seven-year-old James Joyce was the driving force behind the Volta. While in Trieste (then part of the Austro-Hungarian Empire) Joyce's sister had mentioned to him that there was no cinema in Dublin. Joyce, who was always short of funds and still unrecognised as a writer, with two young children and a partner to provide for, seized on the idea as a business project. He visited Dublin in 1909 and took two Triestine businessmen technicians with him: Messers Novak and Lesnardon. He found the ideal site at 45 Mary Street, which had previously been an ironmonger's premises.

Volta Cinema, Mary
Street.

After Joyce advertised for the position of
projectionist, he began interviewing prospective
employees. My grandfather, Lennie Collinge, who
had recently qualified as an electrician, applied for
the position and was interviewed. Since he had a little
French (neither Novak nor Lesnardon spoke English,
but both spoke French), which he had learnt in James's
Street Christian Brothers School, and had a very
outgoing manner, he was successful in the interview.

When the Volta opened it was resplendent in
crimson and light-blue paint. There was huge interest
in the new cinema, with long queues forming outside
and 'sandwich men' (men who wore placards front and
back for advertising purposes) walking about Mary
Street. Later, sandwich men would appear in Joyce's
Ulysses, advertising for Hely's of Dame Street.

Since most of the silent films shown were
either Italian or French, handouts with the English
translation of the intertitles were provided for the
audiences. Films shown included *Beatrice Cenci*, *The
Enchanted Palace* and *Devilled Crab*, as well as films
starring the Chaplinesque comedian Tontolini.

When asked what Joyce was like to work for, my grandfather described him as a tall, thin young man, quiet spoken, who was never to the forefront of cinema business. He seldom engaged in conversation. But my grandfather recalled one particular occasion when he did. This was when my grandfather and his colleagues were discussing the sandwich men. Most of them thought that the job was very demeaning, but Joyce disagreed. He contended that any work, however menial, was preferable to being idle.

Interest in the cinema was intense initially, but soon Dubliners began to realise that the films being shown bore no relation to their lives, and the attendance numbers dropped off. Joyce's business project ground to a halt and he returned to Trieste. The Volta was then taken over by the British Provincial Cinema Company. Renamed the Lyceum, it continued operating in Dublin until 1948, but the number of cinema seats was reduced from six hundred to four hundred.

In 1976, when my grandfather was in his eighties, he opened the exhibition *Cinema Ireland*, organised by the cinema archivist Liam O'Leary. When it was discovered that he had been Joyce's projectionist, he was feted by Joycean scholars, including David Norris, and was interviewed by CBS and RTÉ. He opened Bloomsday at the Joyce Tower in Sandycove in 1979, shortly before his death that same year at the age of ninety. His photo can be seen in the Joyce Museum, as can a ticket for the Volta Cinema with the following inscription below it: 'Lennie Collinge (1889–1979) projectionist at the Volta and student of the master.'

While writing my juvenilia, my former college lecturer, the late Dr Nuala Ó Faoláin, academic and author, asked me if I would consider writing a poem about my grandfather, employing projection as a metaphor. Using cinematic terms throughout, the following poem was the result.

Lennie and Joyce

(*To my grandfather who died in December 1979, aged ninety*)

He always spoke of how
he worked with Joyce,
learning his up and coming
trade, beaming
Dublin's first images of cinema
in the Volta.

Small talk with the master
was his enlarger:
a Liberties man,
he knew his pictures well
and spooled them to the full.

As I serve my time,
I hear the man in the box
drawl Joyce into my ear
and I project the unbroken
beam, over the faceless crowd
onto the page.

Slats the MGM Lion from Dublin

Metro-Goldwyn-Mayer logo featuring Slats, 1926.

Trained by the famous animal trainer Volney Phifer, Slats was born in Dublin Zoo in 1919. Between 1924 and 1928 this lion appeared on the logo of all black-and-white MGM films. The director–publicist Howard Dietz chose a lion because this had been the motto of the athletics team at Columbia University, which he'd attended as an undergraduate and whose fight song was 'roar lion roar!' He is also accredited with using the motto *Ars gratia artis* ('Art for the sake of art'). Slats did not roar, unlike the lions which were later used by MGM, but it was immaterial, as the early MGM films were all silent until the first 'talkie' movie was released by Warner Brothers in 1927. Many other lions were later included on the MGM logo but none from Dublin.

CHAPTER 9

A Terrible Beauty is Born – 1916

In the early twentieth century British rule was still strong in Ireland, especially in Dublin, the second city of the British Empire. Since the loss of the Irish parliament after the Act of Union in 1801, political power was concentrated in Dublin Castle, over which the Lord Lieutenant presided and from which the chief secretary administered. The city was marked by a diversity of class and culture, with a rich merchant elite enjoying an affluent lifestyle while a large underclass

O'Connell Bridge, 1900s.

barely subsisted in the crowded tenements of the inner city – formerly the splendid Georgian houses of the eighteenth-century Anglo-Irish aristocracy. The time was ripe for industrial unrest, and this exploded in 1913 in a series of strikes culminating in the Lockout and the formation of the Irish Citizen Army.

The city was changing rapidly also, as the leafy suburbs expanded and horse-drawn vehicles began to give way to mechanised transport, with trams and motor cars appearing on Dublin streets. The formation of the Irish Volunteers in 1913 in response to the Ulster Volunteers of 1912 meant that its members came from such diverse organisations as the Ancient Order of Hibernians, the Gaelic League, Sinn Féin and the secret Irish Republican Brotherhood.

By 1914 and the outbreak of World War I, the Volunteers split between those who followed John Redmond's advice and joined the British army and those who were bitterly opposed to this strategy, culminating in the 1916 Rising, then referred to as the 'Sinn Féin rebellion'. This would lead to the deaths of 485 people, including civilians, British soldiers and police as well as Irish rebels. Irish history had been 'changed utterly' – to quote the poet W.B. Yeats.

Rosie Hackett

Rosie Hackett was born in a tenement on Bolton Street, Dublin, one of a family of six children. Her father, John Hackett, died when Rosie was young and her mother remarried, after which the family moved to Old Abbey Street. At sixteen years of age, Hackett joined the Irish Transport and General Workers' Union (ITGWU), which was founded by Jim Larkin in 1909. She would go on to be involved in trade union activity for the rest of her life. As a packer in Jacob's biscuit factory, she organised in favour of the male workers who had come out on strike and managed to secure better working conditions and a pay rise. Two

years later she and Delia Larkin (Jim Larkin's sister) founded the Irish Women Workers' Union (IWWU).

During the 1913 Lockout, Hackett mobilised the workers in Jacob's to come out on strike in sympathy with their fellow workers and she was active in the running of soup kitchens in Liberty Hall to feed the strikers. By 1914 she had been fired from her job in Jacob's.

Hackett later worked as a clerk in the printshop of Liberty Hall, where she became a member of the Irish Citizen Army. This saw her on active service during the 1916 Rising, fighting alongside Countess Markievicz in the College of Surgeons. She helped print the Proclamation of the Republic, which she handed over to James Connolly before Patrick Pearse read it out on the steps of the GPO.

A year after Connolly's execution, Hackett and her colleagues in the ITGWU hung a banner from Liberty Hall proclaiming that Connolly had been murdered. The police quickly took down the banner,

Women Workers' Union, Liberty Hall, c.1914. Reproduced courtesy of the National Library of Ireland.

Liberty Hall, *c.1917.*

but Rosie and three female colleagues made a second one. Having nailed the doors shut upstairs in Liberty Hall, they hung the banner and resisted police efforts to take it down.

After the 1916 Rising Hackett was still active in the IWWU and by 1945 had secured extra holiday time for laundry workers. Having served the trade union movement for fifty years, she was awarded a gold medal. Rosie Hackett never married and lived in Fairview with her brother until her death in 1976 at the age of eighty-three.

In 2014 the Rosie Hackett Bridge, named in her honour, was opened by the Lord Mayor of Dublin. The bridge is 26 metres wide and 48 metres long – it spans the River Liffey and joins Marlborough Street to Hawkins Street. It is open to public transport, cyclists and pedestrians.

The 1916 Rising

Dubliner Roddy Doyle, novelist, dramatist and screenwriter, has won many awards and has had many of his books made into films. He is most famous for his Barrytown Trilogy and the comic dialogue of the Dublin characters.

In his novel *A Star Called Henry*, Roddy tells the story of Henry Sharpe who, at only fourteen years of age, is already six feet two inches in height. A member of the Irish Citizen Army, he and his colleagues storm the GPO on Easter Monday 1916.

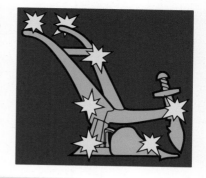

The original Starry Plough flag of the Irish Citizen Army, 1914.

From *A Star Called Henry*

Then I heard Connolly's voice.

—The GPO charge!

And I ran. The hammers jumped on my shoulder, the rifle smacked my back. A few of the men fired into the air. I ran past Plunkett who was being held up by Collins and another officer, his arms around their necks, two enormous rings on his fingers. For a second I thought he'd been shot – there was blood seeping through a bandage on his neck – and I ducked, half expecting to be knocked back by a bullet. But I looked back and I saw the signs; I'd seen them on Victor and thousands of others: the man had T.B. I ran into the main hall and my boots joined the chaos, in time to see the remaining shock on the faces of staff and customers.

Again Connolly was in charge.

—Everyone out!

Some of the staff, men who hadn't exerted themselves in years, hopped and skidded over the counter.

—Jesus will you look at them, said Paddy Swanzy.
—Men, women and children first.

And now, only a few minutes later, Pearse and Connolly were about to go back outside, and Clarke with them. We heard cheering: the crowd across the street was watching the green, white and orange flag of the Republic being hoisted to the top of the flagpole above us. They clapped and cheered. I pictured the flag being caught by the wind and opened, colour by colour. And Countess Markievicz's bedspread was flying up there as well, with its gold and mustard lettering – *Irish Republic*. I cheered too; I couldn't help it.

The GPO, Sackville Street (O'Connell Street), in the aftermath of the 1916 Rising. *Reproduced courtesy of the National Library of Ireland.*

Connolly, Pearse and Clarke went out. I couldn't see them now but I soon heard Pearse.

—He's reading it, I whispered.

—Reading what?

—*The Sacred Heart Messenger*, said Paddy Swanzy.

—Shush in the ranks!

We declare the right of the people of Ireland to the ownership of Ireland, and to the unfettered control of Irish destinies, to be sovereign and indefeasible. There was jeering and laughter, small spells of applause, but at times as he read there wasn't a noise. And his voice was soft; it drifted in the heat, barely there. The men with me were hearing the Proclamation for the first time. I watched their faces as the words rolled up to them. I watched the pride and excitement. I saw eyes shine and moisten ... *We hereby proclaim the Irish Republic as a Sovereign Independent State, and we pledge our lives and the lives of our comrades-in-arms to the cause of its freedom.*

Paddy Swanzy hadn't said a word in at least a minute.

—Them's fighting words, he said.

The Republic guarantees religious and civil liberty

—Go home!

—Go home yourself. Let the man speak.

and declares its resolve to pursue the happiness and prosperity of the whole nation and all its parts, cherishing all the children of the nation equally. ...

We place the cause of the Irish Republic under the protection of the Most High God, Whose blessing we invoke upon our arms, and we pray that no one who serves that cause will dishonour it by cowardice, inhumanity or rapine. ...

Pearse and Connolly came back in and the big doors were shut with a resounding thump that left us still for a few seconds. Then men started to tear down the recruitment posters – *The Irishmen in the Trenches are calling for YOU* – and put Proclamations in their place. The building and waiting continued. And Kitchener and George V were put propping up one of the barricades; someone had fecked[1] them from the Waxworks around the corner on Henry Street. The far-off gunfire was still sprinkling the city.

1 Stolen.

Connolly did the rounds. He terrified all of us. He walloped one of the window barriers. Wood and paper fell to the floor.

—What use is that to us? he shouted. —Will that thing stop bullets? Some of us aren't playing here, you know. I want barricades.

He sent men running, grown men scampering. They loved and feared him. He was sharp, always on the prowl, never ever happy. But everything he did and said, everything he slammed, lambasted, everything he was, was for us. And the men knew it. He came growling over to my barricade and tapped it with his foot. It stayed put, except for a loose page that fluttered out the window. He winked at me and moved on.

—Here come the military!

The call came from outside and it ricocheted from walls to ceiling of the main hall and upstairs to the other men and sent feet punching the boards and tiles, and officers shouting across each other. I climbed onto the bench we'd put against the barricade and watched for the arrival of the enemy. My rifle roamed the street, followed the retreating onlookers, searched for creeping men in khaki. A few people stayed behind, under the Pillar, including a family with a dog on a string. And there were some perched up on the lampposts. There were priests out there too, in black stovepipe hats, moving in a row, trying to disperse the crowd. They were wasting their time. The crowd let them through and immediately re-gathered. ...

I was ready. At last. I aimed at Tyler's window.

I heard the first shot crack brick. And then I fired. I heard, then saw the shop glass break and disappear as the trigger threw my finger forward. I pulled back the bolt, the empty cartridge flew over my shoulder. I grabbed the trigger back and fired at the exposed boots and slippers. Then I fired at Noblett's window and the cakes and cream jumped out of their stands. O'Farrell's. The glass fell onto the tobacco and cigars. ...

I shot and killed all that I had been denied, all the commerce and snobbery that had been mocking me and other hundreds of thousands behind glass and locks, all the injustice, unfairness and shoes – while the lads took chunks out of the military.

They drove their bullets into the dragoons – the Sixth Reserve Cavalry Regiment from Marlborough Barracks, I found out years later when I was comforting one of the widows – and their fat gleaming steeds. By the time I was finished with the shop windows there were horses, dead or twitching, lying all over Upper Sackville Street and their riders were under them or hobbling and crawling away back up towards Cavendish Row. Their bullets still pinged and skipped and the street-sides tossed back the echoes. I aimed at a chap who'd lost his helmet, whose face was cut in half by a moustache with ends standing up like black candles. He looked stranded out there, trying to control his horse and hold on to his lance; the horse was spinning on its hind legs, propelled by its terror. I waited until horse and rider gave me their side view again. Then I let go of a bullet that went through the rider's leg and the horse dropped flat onto the street.

W.B. Yeats

Irish poet and Nobel laureate W.B. Yeats (1865–1939) was in London when the Easter Rising took place.

It was reported that he was a little upset that he had not been 'consulted' beforehand. His iconic poem 'Easter 1916' eulogises the leaders of the rebellion, but Yeats writes not of a terrible violence being born, but of 'a terrible beauty'. He had previously despaired of idealism when he wrote 'Romantic Ireland's dead and gone', but here the poet shows a change of heart, implying that the self-sacrifice of the leaders has immortalised them in the pantheon of Irish heroes.

W.B. Yeats by John Singer Sargent.

Easter 1916

I have met them at close of day
Coming with vivid faces
From counter or desk among grey
Eighteenth-century houses.
I have passed with a nod of the head
Or polite meaningless words,
Or have lingered awhile and said
Polite meaningless words,
And thought before I had done
Of a mocking tale or a gibe
To please a companion
Around the fire at the club,
Being certain that they and I
But lived where motley is worn:
All changed, changed utterly:
A terrible beauty is born.

That woman's days were spent
In ignorant good-will,
Her nights in argument
Until her voice grew shrill.
What voice more sweet than hers
When, young and beautiful,
She rode to harriers?

Birth of the Irish Republic by Walter Paget, *c.*1918.

This man had kept a school
And rode our wingèd horse;
This other his helper and friend
Was coming into his force;
He might have won fame in the end,
So sensitive his nature seemed,
So daring and sweet his thought.
This other man I had dreamed
A drunken, vainglorious lout.
He had done most bitter wrong
To some who are near my heart,
Yet I number him in the song;
He, too, has resigned his part
In the casual comedy;
He, too, has been changed in his turn,
Transformed utterly:
A terrible beauty is born.

Hearts with one purpose alone
Through summer and winter seem
Enchanted to a stone
To trouble the living stream.
The horse that comes from the road,
The rider, the birds that range
From cloud to tumbling cloud,
Minute by minute they change;

A shadow of cloud on the stream
Changes minute by minute;
A horse-hoof slides on the brim,
And a horse plashes within it;
The long-legged moor-hens dive,
And hens to moor-cocks call;
Minute by minute they live:
The stone's in the midst of all.

Too long a sacrifice
Can make a stone of the heart.
O when may it suffice?
That is Heaven's part, our part
To murmur name upon name,
As a mother names her child
When sleep at last has come
On limbs that had run wild.
What is it but nightfall?
No, no, not night but death;
Was it needless death after all?
For England may keep faith
For all that is done and said.
We know their dream; enough
To know they dreamed and are dead;
And what if excess of love
Bewildered them till they died?
I write it out in a verse –
MacDonagh and MacBride
And Connolly and Pearse
Now and in time to be,
Wherever green is worn,
Are changed, changed utterly:
A terrible beauty is born.

Civilian Casualties

I wrote this piece and read it for a live broadcast of
Sunday Miscellany from the stage of the Wexford Opera
House in 2016 as part of the RTÉ commemoration of
the 1916 Rising.

Rosanna Heffernan, Casualty of War

In our family lore the 1916 Rising bulked large: my late father, although only three years of age at the time, recalled how a trip to Sandymount Strand with his mother and two-year-old brother Bertie, in the glorious sunshine of that Easter Monday, was cancelled after a young man entered the Iveagh Buildings in the Liberties where they lived, screaming, 'The rebels are in the Post Office! The rebels are in the Post Office!'

My late mother often spoke of her father, Laurence Greene, who had gone to Howth with his wheelbarrow to unload the consignment of old German Mauser rifles from the *Asgard* in the summer of 1914.

More poignant, however, was the tragic death of my great-grandmother, Rosanna Heffernan, who became an early civilian casualty on Tuesday, 25 April 1916.

Since my details of her were limited to what my grandmother had told me and since I had seen no photos of her, I accessed the 1911 census to find her and her husband Hugh in 176 James's Street. Her husband died later that same year. In addition to her four young adult children, she kept lodgers, as the house was a three-storey building. Interestingly, her neighbour was W.T. Cosgrave, who lived over the pub at 174 James's Street and both he and his half-bother Frank were in the Volunteers.

On Easter Monday 1916 the South Dublin Union was seized and occupied by Volunteers under the command of Commandant Éamonn Ceannt and Vice Commandant Cathal Brugha. The Volunteers came under attack from soldiers of the Royal Irish Regiment and staff and civilians alike were caught up in the exchange as the sudden occupation of the buildings prevented a full-scale evacuation.

As the Royal Irish Regiment approached they were fired on by Volunteers from this complex. In an effort to lay down covering fire for Sherwood Foresters who were advancing towards the South Dublin Union, a British army machine-gun post on the roof of the Royal Hospital

Sinn Fein Rebellion, 1916. Sackville Street, Dublin.

in Kilmainham was later trained on the Volunteers who had occupied the nurses' quarters.

On Tuesday morning, 25 April, during the exchange, a bullet smashed through the upper window of 176 James's Street and ricocheted off the metal Sacred Heart oil lamp on the wall. Rosanna Heffernan, now fifty-five years of age, who had ironically ushered two of her lodgers upstairs to safer quarters when the firing began, was hit in the neck. As her family rushed to her side, she uttered her last words: 'Sweet heart of Jesus have mercy on my soul.' She died two days later in Steeven's Hospital. W.T. Cosgrave's half-brother, Frank, also died on 25 April in the exchange with the Royal Irish Regiment.

Rosanna's young married daughter, Mary, my grandmother, braved gunfire that day to go out and buy a shroud, but when the family went to the hospital to reclaim the body, it was hastily buried in the grounds of the hospital.

After the Civil War ended in May 1923, Volunteers who had seen action were rewarded with state pensions but there was no compensation available to the Heffernan family for the loss of their mother or the fracture of their entire family. On reflection, it is quite possible that the bullet which killed Rosanna was fired from one of the

Sackville Street (O'Connell Street), 1916. *Reproduced courtesy of the National Library of Ireland.*

very Mauser rifles that my grandfather Laurence Greene had carried from Howth two years earlier in 1914, inadvertently causing the death of his own mother-in-law while, ironically, bullets fired by her neighbour W.T. Cosgrave and his colleagues in the South Dublin Union could also have accounted for her death. Such is the cruel irony of conflict.

The military historian Conor Dodd, of the Glasnevin Trust, kindly emailed me a newspaper report of my great-grandmother's death and a photograph. It shows an Edwardian woman who looks hauntingly at the camera without smiling. The same photo also appears in Joe Duffy's book *Children of the Rising*.

This year, as we celebrate the hundredth anniversary of 1916, I fondly remember my great-grandmother, Rosanna Heffernan, from Kilbeggan, County Westmeath, who bore six children, five of whom survived, and who died tragically at fifty-five years of age. I recall this woman from whom we inherited our dark skin and brown eyes, her poignant last words and my late mother, Rosanna, who proudly carried her name for her own ninety-three years. In Sean O'Casey's play *Shadow of a Gunman* the cynical Seamus Shields states: 'it's the civilians that suffer ... Shot in the back to save the British Empire, an' shot in the breast to save the soul of Ireland.'

Civilians killed in the 1916 Rising, who account for 54 per cent of fatalities, surely deserve to be remembered and celebrated also in the pantheon of modern Irish history.

CHAPTER 10

Poet Stories

From as far back as the twelfth century in Ireland the professional Gaelic poet held a place of esteem in Irish society. By the early eighteenth century, however, as the old Gaelic order collapsed and English became the dominant vernacular, the poets fell on hard times and could no longer live on the generosity of their patrons. By the nineteenth and twentieth centuries Irish poets recovered sufficiently to hold their own in Irish society and Nobel laureate W.B. Yeats, in 'Under Ben Bulben' (1933), advised as follows:

Celtic bard depicted in a nineteenth-century engraving.

> Irish poets learn your trade
> Sing whatever is well made ...
> Sing the peasantry, and then
> Hard-riding country gentlemen,
> The holiness of monks, and after
> Porter-drinkers' randy laughter ...

Poets such as Austin Clarke, Patrick Kavanagh, Thomas Kinsella and John Montague would follow his lead, culminating in Seamus Heaney being awarded the Nobel Prize in Literature in 1995.

During the late 1970s and early 1980s, the young Dermot Bolger organised poetry readings and workshops in the Grapevine Arts Centre in North Great George's Street. As a participant, I met such writers as Patrick McCabe and Michael O'Loughlin. I learned also that the war poet Francis Ledwidge (1887–1917) had not only inspired me to write creatively in my early teens but had also inspired Dermot Bolger, who went on the distinguish himself as a poet, author and playwright.

Francis Ledwidge.

From Rathfarnham to Slane: Francis Ledwidge, Stolen Pigeons and Juvenilia

Francis Ledwidge (1887–1918), who became known as 'the poet of the blackbird', had been born to a farm labourer in Slane, County Meath. He left school at thirteen and worked on local farms. He also worked, seasonally, as a road worker and later in a local copper mine. Dismissed from this job for organising a strike, he was sent to Rathfarnham in Dublin by his mother to train as an apprentice grocer. At sixteen years of age the young Ledwidge was terribly homesick. He sat up into the small hours and wrote his first poem, entitled 'Behind the Closed Eye'.

Behind the Closed Eye
I walk the old frequented ways
That wind around the tangled braes,
I live again the sunny days
Ere I the city knew.

And scenes of old again are born,
The woodbine lassoing the thorn,
And drooping Ruth-like in the corn
The poppies weep the dew.

Above me in their hundred schools
The magpies bend their young to rules,
And like an apron full of jewels
The dewy cobweb swings.

And frisking in the stream below
The troutlets make the circles flow,
And the hungry crane doth watch them grow
As a smoker does his rings.

Above me smokes the little town,
With its whitewashed walls and roofs of brown
And its octagon spire toned smoothly down
As the holy minds within.

And wondrous impudently sweet,
Half of him passion, half conceit,
The blackbird calls adown the street
Like the piper of Hamelin.

Main Street,
Rathfarnham,
1900–20. *Reproduced
courtesy of the National
Library of Ireland.*

Thomas McDonagh.

Joseph Mary Plunkett.

Patrick Pearse.

I hear him, and I feel the lure
Drawing me back to the homely moor,
I'll go and close the mountain's door
On the city's strife and din.

Elated by the completion of his first poem, Ledwidge decided to leave the grocery store and trek the entire forty miles back to Slane. He rested along the route at every milestone. Although a committed nationalist, ten years later, in 1914, Ledwidge enlisted in the British army. 'I joined the British Army because she stood between Ireland and an enemy common to our civilization and I would not have her say that she defended us while we did nothing at home but pass resolutions.'

Francis Ledwidge was killed during World War I when a shell exploded as he was road-building in Flanders. After his death in 1918 many of his poems were published by his friend and fellow poet Lord Dunsany – among them the following tribute to the poet leaders of the 1916 Rising such as Thomas McDonagh, Joseph Mary Plunkett and Patrick Pearse.

Lament for the Poets
I heard the Poor Old Woman say:
'At break of day the fowler came,
And took my blackbirds from their songs
Who loved me well thro' shame and blame.

No more from lovely distances
Their songs shall bless me mile by mile,
Nor to white Ashbourne call me down
To wear my crown another while.

With bended flowers the angels mark
For the skylark the place they lie,
From there its little family
Shall dip their wings first in the sky.

And when the first surprise of flight
Sweet songs excite, from the far dawn
Shall there come blackbirds loud with love,
Sweet echoes of the singers gone.

But in the lovely hush of eve
Weeping I grieve the silent bills,'
I heard the Poor Old Woman say
In Derry of the little hills.

As a thirteen-year-old student, I studied this poem in school and was told by our teacher that the poem was, in fact, an allegory: that the Poor Old Woman was Ireland personified and that the blackbirds represented the executed poets.

I was a young pigeon-fancier at the time, with a small loft of homing pigeons in my back garden in Walkinstown. One night some thugs broke into the loft, stole my small flock and left the door open for a neighbour's cat to kill the remaining nestlings below in the nest boxes. I was very upset, although I was consoled a little when, a few days later, some pigeons returned to the loft.

I was determined to celebrate the birds that had been stolen or killed so, one night while in bed, I began to compose a lament entitled 'The Stolen Pigeons'. Since I had learnt Ledwidge's 'Lament for the Poets' off by heart this became my template:

A poor pigeon lover said
'And I in bed the schemers came
And took my pigeons from their loft
With thoughts of theft and greed in head.'

Ledwidge's metre, based, as it was, on Irish syllabic poems, was difficult to sustain but I did my best – ending the poem as follows:

We may have pigeons better bred
Who for their price we may think cheap
But the memory we'll always keep
Of the mealy, pair and little red.

Undeterred that I had plagiarised Ledwidge's poem, I jumped out of bed and rummaged in the dressing-table drawer until I had found a pen and paper on which to jot down my first poem before I had forgotten the lines. I experienced a sense of elation as I viewed the words dancing on the copy page.

The following day I proudly showed the poem to my English teacher. He was impressed and asked me then if I wanted to be a poet when I was older. I replied that I wanted to teach, and he reminded me that many a good poet had also been a teacher, but he did warn me that neither poet nor teacher were often appreciated by the general public.

At sixteen years of age, Dermot Bolger read Alice Curtayne's fine biography of Frances Ledwidge. Then while writing his juvenilia, and hoping to become a successful poet, he retraced some of the route that Ledwidge had taken on his long hike back to Slane. There was one surviving milestone. There Dermot would sit, thinking of Ledwidge and hoping that his spirit might give him the reassurance he so vitally needed – even if subliminally. He was convinced that if he made that same journey back to the cottage in Slane, he would experience something of the dead poet's sensibility.

At twenty years of age, Dermot did make the 'pilgrimage' to the cottage in Slane – only to be frisked by the local garda sergeant who thought the long-haired young man was a burglar! Once his credentials were established, the garda was very helpful. Dermot was directed to the derelict cottage, his pilgrimage complete. In years to come he would base his play *Walking the Road* on Ledwidge's walk as a boy, and he would also edit *The Ledwidge Treasury*, containing the war poet's selected poems.

In the summer of 2007 Dermot Bolger, his late wife, Bernie, and their sons, Donnacha and Diarmuid, joined my wife, Margaret, and me for drinks in the Parknasilla Hotel. Here he and I discussed our common interest in Francis Ledwidge and how that poet had inspired our juvenilia. I wrote the following poem, which became even more poignant since Bernie died suddenly in 2010. It is now displayed in the Parknasilla Hotel.

Parknasilla Hotel August 2007
(*In fond memory of Bernie Bolger*)

Caha Mountains, County Kerry.

The water shone like cruets on the
    bay
the Caha Hills episcopal in purple
as we lingered among rhododendron
    walks
and strolled on sandstone bossed
    with limpets.

Here the ticking of clocks becomes irrelevant,
of no more consequence than the breaking waves,
where indolence is justified and the measured
flapping of grey herons becomes our sole template.

By night the virtuosity of piano and strings
unravelling taut nerves as the spirit glow
suffusing faces, spreads in common purpose
reducing differences to one fond voice.

To the east the little nest of Kenmare[1]
warms its clutch while further west
the little knot of Sneem clings fast[2]
to hold us as we drift beyond our time.

When my new and selected poems were published in 2013, I named the collection *The Lonely Hush of Eve*, recalling the lines from Ledwidge which had inspired

1   The Irish language name for Kenmare is Neidín, meaning 'little nest'.

2   The Irish language name for Sneem is An tSnaidhm, meaning 'the knot'.

my first poem. The next poem, entitled 'Road Building', recalls the conversation in the Parknasilla Hotel.

Road Building – A Tribute to Francis Ledwidge
(*For Dermot Bolger*)

You walk before us still in the hush of eve,
a young man in khaki, mud-spattered from
road-building, retracing your steps to Slane.

You sang for me when I delivered
my infant poem and, in the chords and
internal rhyme, I proudly glossed

four hundred years of Bardic gold,
honed since the first blackbird gilded
branches, to lament my stolen pigeons.

On another journey a young man walked
in your footsteps, retracing each milestone
to an uncertain future beyond Finglas.

We have realised your stolen years,
have seen the Dark Cow leave the moor,
but still you beckon us on to build and build,

with pick and shovel, roads not travelled,
things that never were, ways uncharted
in cyberspace, whose goal is still delight;

In the comfort of a southern hotel
we share your youthful dreams, brought at last
to fruition in our middle years;

You place your hands on our shoulders,
look calm as the day you built your last road,
walk from us, slowly, to the homely moor.

Among the Faceless Throng:
Mairtín Ó Direáin

Mairtín Ó Direáin (1919–88) was
born on Inishmore, one of the Aran
Islands, off the west coast of Ireland
in 1910. In 1928 he left Aran to work
in the Galway post office and from
there moved to Dublin, where he
worked in the civil service until his
retirement. He is widely regarded
as one of the foremost Irish language poets of the   Inishmore.
twentieth century. While his early poems express a
nostalgia for Aran, his later poems measure the values
of the contemporary Irish nation by the yardstick
of Inishmore, and generally find them wanting. His
poetry was regularly prescribed for study by Irish
students in secondary school, with such poems as 'An
tEarrach Thiar' (spring in the west), 'Dínit an Bhróin'
(the dignity of grief) and 'Stoite' (uprooted) to the
fore. While he was often critical of Dublin, he was
happy to live for most of his life in a bungalow on
Whitehall Road in south Dublin with his wife, Áine,
and daughter, Niamh.

The following two poems are set in Dublin, the
first expressing Ó Direáin's anger at a gull which left
a 'present' on his head, where the poet uses the gull
to represent the more mercenary, greedy elements of
society, and the swan to represent nobility and integrity.
The second poem suggests that were his ghost to return
few would be frightened, as Irish language poets are
seldom well-known among English speakers.

Faoileán Drochmhúinte

Is a liacht fear is ban
In Átha Cliath cois Life,
Tuige duit, a chladhaire
Féirín a scaoileadh ar fhile?

Coinnigh do phráib agat féin,
A éin an chraois bhradaigh,
Is le do mharthain arís
An file seo ná salaigh.

Leor mar léan liom
Go bhfeicim go seasta
Gur líonmhar d'ál
Ná pór ard na heala

Ill-Mannered Gull
Of all the men and women
In Dublin by the Liffey
Why, you scoundrel,
Did you bestow a gift on a poet?

Keep your filth to yourself
You voracious devious bird
And never besmear
This poet again while you live.

It's surely sad enough for me
That I steadily see
Your breed outstripping
The noble seed of the swan.

(*Translated by Declan Collinge*)

Mo Thaibhse
Mo thaibhse dá dtagadh an treo
Níos faide anonn san aimsir
Is séarsa aonair a thabhairt
Bóthar an Dún Ghoirt is thairis
Go Bóthar Thí Mológ ar aistear,
Le neach de Chlann an Bhéarla
Mó chló níorbh ionadh,
Mo bhás dá mb'eol dóibh
An tásc níor chás leo:
Ní foláir nó is taibhse mé

I meabhair an tsóirt sin cheana:
Leo is neamhní mo bheo ná mo mhairbh.

My Ghost
Were my ghost to pass this way
At a future time
Hurrying down
Fortfield Road and
Travelling on to Templeogue Road
No English speaker would be surprised,
Even if they knew I was dead
It would not bother them.
I'm surely already a ghost
To those of that mind:
They are not concerned about me living or dead.

(*Translated by Declan Collinge*)

Katharine Tynan

Clondalkin-born Katharine Tynan (1859–1931) was a friend of W.B. Yeats and Gerard Manley Hopkins. Besides writing poetry she wrote over a hundred novels. She lived in Dublin until her marriage to the English barrister Henry Albert Hinkson in 1893, but they returned briefly to Ireland, living in Mayo for four years before returning to England.

A walk in the Dublin Mountains in spring is said to be the occasion which inspired the following poem. A Celtic cross on Belgard Road, Tallaght, can be still seen today. This commemorates Katharine's father whose dairy farm was in this area. The road, which runs between the estates of Kilnamanagh and Kingswood in Tallaght to reach the Belgard Road, is now called Katharine Tynan Road. My sister Maura once recited this poem in the Feis.

Katharine Tynan.
Reproduced courtesy of the National Library of Ireland.

Sheep and Lambs

All in the April evening,
April airs were abroad;
The sheep with their little lambs
Pass'd me by on the road.

The sheep with their little lambs
Pass'd me by on the road;
All in the April evening
I thought on the Lamb of God.

The lambs were weary and crying
With a weak, human cry.
I thought on the Lamb of God
Going meekly to die.

Up in the blue, blue mountains
Dewy pastures are sweet:
Rest for the little bodies,
Rest for the little feet.

But for the Lamb of God,
Up on the hill-top green,
Only a Cross of shame
Two stark crosses between.

All in the April evening,
April airs were abroad;
I saw the sheep with their lambs,
And thought on the Lamb of God.

Two Dublin Poems by Patrick Kavanagh

Monaghan poet Patrick Kavanagh (1904–67) settled in
Dublin in 1939 and remained there until his death. In
1944, while staying on Raglan Road in Dublin, he met
and fell in love with the beautiful twenty-two-year-
old Hilda Moriarty, a medical student from Kerry.
Initially flattered at the attention of the forty-year-old
poet, she eventually tired of his company, especially
since he followed her round the city even when she
was with her friends.

'On Raglan Road', first published in 1946, was set to the music of 'The Dawning of the Day', a traditional Irish air, and it was best sung by Luke Kelly of the Dubliners. Kavanagh suggests in the poem that he was too important a poet to have associated with an ordinary girl, despite her beauty! ('When the angel woos the clay he'd lose his wings at the dawn of day.') The third line of the first verse is regularly misquoted as 'I saw the danger and I walked' rather than '… yet I walked'.

Luke Kelly by John Coll, South King Street.

On Raglan Road

On Raglan Road on an autumn day I met her first and
  knew
That her dark hair would weave a snare that I might
  one day rue;
I saw the danger, yet I walked along the enchanted
  way,
And I said, let grief be a fallen leaf at the dawning of
  the day.

On Grafton Street in November we tripped lightly
  along the ledge
Of the deep ravine where can be seen the worth of
  passion's pledge,
The Queen of Hearts still making tarts and I not
  making hay –
O I loved too much and by such, by such, is
  happiness thrown away.

I gave her gifts of the mind, I gave her the secret sign
  that's known
To the artists who have known the true gods of
  sound and stone
And word and tint. I did not stint for I gave her
  poems to say
With her own name there and her own dark hair like
  clouds over fields of May

On a quiet street where old ghosts meet I see her
    walking now
Away from me so hurriedly my reason must allow
That I had wooed not as I should a creature made of
    clay –
When the angel woos the clay he'd lose his wings at
    the dawn of day.

Patrick Kavanagh
by John Coll, Grand
Canal.

Having had a cancerous lung removed, Kavanagh was given a new lease of life. He wrote the following sonnet in 1955 after walking regularly along the banks of the Grand Canal, resolving to enjoy the simplest things around him and to relish merely being alive. A bronze statue of the poet by the sculptor John Coll can now be seen on Mespil Road on the north bank of the Grand Canal.

Canal Bank Walk

Leafy-with-love banks and the green waters of the
    canal
Pouring redemption for me, that I do
The will of God, wallow in the habitual, the banal,
Grow with nature again as before I grew.
The bright stick trapped, the breeze adding a third
Party to the couple kissing on an old seat,
And a bird gathering materials for the nest for the
    Word,
Eloquently new and abandoned to its delirious beat.
O unworn world enrapture me, encapture me in a
    web
Of fabulous grass and eternal voices by a beech,
Feed the gaping need of my senses, give me ad lib
To pray unselfconsciously with overflowing speech,
For this soul needs to be honoured with a new dress
    woven
From green and blue things and arguments that
    cannot be proven.

CHAPTER 11
Down by Anna Liffey

The River Liffey runs 78 miles (125 kilometres) from its source between Kippure and Tonduff in the Wicklow Mountains to its mouth in Dublin Bay. It runs through the streets of Dublin before it enters the sea. While its main tributaries are the rivers Dodder, Poddle and Camac, it has many smaller tributaries such as Athdown Brook, Shankill River, Rye Water and Glenaulin Stream. The river has inspired countless songs and poems, from James Joyce's 'Anna Livia Plurabelle' in *Finnegans Wake* to Peadar Kearney's 'Down by the Liffeyside'. Brendan Behan quipped,

Sarah's Bridge on the River Anna Liffey, 1837.

Dublin City, 2022.

'Somebody once said that "Joyce has made of this river the Ganges of the literary world" but sometimes the smell of the Ganges of the literary world is not all that literary!'

The Liffey Swim

The Liffey Swim is an annual swimming race in the River Liffey in Dublin, over a distance of one and a half miles (2.2 kilometres). It has been held every year since 1920 in late August or early September, with the hundredth race taking place in 2019.

Initially the Liffey Swim was only open to men, in no small part due to the late archbishop of Dublin John Charles McQuaid (1895–1973), who discouraged women's sporting events. However, since 1977 there has been a women's race also. The highest number of women finishing the race was in 2007, when 115 completed it.

The course of the race has been from Rory O'More Bridge to beyond the Custom House on the North Dock, although in some years it was rerouted due to the health risks posed by pollution. Since the River Liffey often has high levels of E. coli and wetsuits are prohibited, Dublin Fire Brigade provides the swimmers with decontamination showers after the race.

Jack B. Yeats captured the atmosphere of the race in his expressionist painting *The Liffey Swim* in 1923. A viewer of this remarkable work can't help but engage with the spectators as they lean over the riverbank to catch a glimpse of the swimmers nearing the finishing line.

Jessica Traynor

Jessica Traynor is an award-winning poet and creative-writing teacher. A former literary manager of the Abbey Theatre, she has been deputy director for the emigration museum, EPIC. The following poem, from her debut collection, *Liffey Swim* (2014), captures the ambience of the race in more recent times.

Liffey Swim

In the dream, the Blessington Street Basin
fills with the Liffey's stout-bottle waters,
but still the swimmers come, in droves,
on the stray sovereign of an Irish summer's day.

The river courses through the city,
turning concrete roadways to canal banks
that shrug their shoulders into dark water;
a man rises, seal-like in his caul of silt, to wave.

At the sluice gates, where the river bends
out of sight between toppling buildings,
a black dog jumps, again and again, into water.

And there, at the edge of vision, my parents,
ready to join the swimmers,
gesture their cheerful farewells.

Peadar Kearney

Peadar Kearney (1883–1942) was a republican who fought in the 1916 Rising and in the Irish Civil War (1922–23). He was a close friend of Michael Collins. A prolific songwriter, he composed 'Amhrán na bhFiann' (the soldier's song), which is now the Irish

Peadar Kearney, 1912.

national anthem. His sister Kathleen married Stephen Behan. Their son, the writer Brendan Behan, often boasted that 'my uncle wrote the national anthem'. One of Kearney's most famous songs is 'Down by the Liffeyside'. It romantically describes a young Dublin couple falling in love and looking forward to getting married. Both are proud Dubliners and republicans.

Down by the Liffeyside

'Twas down by Anna Liffey, my love and I did stray
Where in the good old slushy mud the sea gulls sport
    and play
We got the whiff of ray and chips and Mary softly
    sighed,
'Oh John, come on for a wan and wan[1]
Down by the Liffeyside.'

Then down along by George's Street the loving pair
    to view
While Mary swanked it like a queen in a skirt of royal
    blue;
Her hat was lately turned and her blouse was newly
    dyed,
Oh you could not match her round the block,
Down by the Liffeyside.

And on her old melodeon how sweetly could she
    play;
'Good-by-ee' and 'Don't sigh-ee' and 'Rule Brittanni-
    ay'
But when she turned Sinn Féiner me heart near burst
    with pride,
To hear her sing the 'Soldier's Song',
Down by the Liffeyside.

1 A one and one – a portion of fish and chips.

On Sunday morning to Meath street together we will
    go,
And it's up to Father Murphy we both will make our
    vow
We'll join our hands in wedlock bands and we'll be
    soon outside
For a whole afternoon, for our honeymoon,
Down by the Liffeyside.

Custom House Quay
in the late nineteenth
century.

CHAPTER 12

Delightfully Coarse – Brendan Behan

Brendan Behan (1923–64), poet, novelist, playwright and raconteur, was one of Dublin's most well-known and colourful modern writers. He grew up in Russell Street in the north inner city, in a staunch republican family: his father, Stephen Behan, had been one of Michael Collins's 'Twelve Apostles', while his mother, Kathleen Kearney, was a sister of Peadar Kearney who composed the Irish national anthem.

Brendan worked as a house painter before becoming involved in the republican movement. He served time in a Borstal (youth prison) in England and later in Mountjoy Prison for his republican activity and went on to write his autobiographical novel *Borstal Boy* and such plays as *The Quare Fellow* and *The Hostage*. His fame and financial success only exacerbated his alcoholism, and he died at the age of forty-one having fallen into a diabetic coma. He is reported to have addressed the religious sister who attended him as follows: 'Sister, may all your sons be bishops!'

Study from life of Brendan Behan by Reginald Gray, 1953.

Brendan Behan Returns to Ireland, 1941

A sixteen-year-old Brendan Behan was arrested in
Liverpool in 1939 for the possession of explosives. He
had joined the IRA that year and was attempting,
single-handedly, to bomb the Liverpool docks.
Although sentenced to three years in Borstal, he was
released in 1941 and deported back to Ireland. In this
excerpt, the concluding section of his autobiographical
novel *Borstal Boy*, he describes his elation at returning
to Dublin.

From *Borstal Boy*

The next morning I stood on the deck while the boat came
into Dun Laoghaire, and looked at the sun struggling out
over the hills; and the city all around the bay.

> ... and I will make my journey, if life and health but
> stand,
> Unto that pleasant country, that fresh and fragrant
> strand,
> And leave your boasted braveries, your wealth and
> high command,
> For the fair hills of Holy Ireland ...[1]

There they were, as if I'd never left them; in their sweet and
stately order round the bay – Bray Head, the Sugarloaf, the
Two Rock, the Three Rock, Kippure, the king of them all,
rising his threatening head behind and over their shoulders
till they sloped down to the city. I counted the spires, from
Rathmines' fat dome on one side of St George's spire on the
north, and in the centre, Christchurch. Among the smaller
ones, just on the docks, I could pick out, even in the haze of
morning, the ones I knew best; St Laurence O'Toole's and
St Barnabas; I had them all counted, present and correct
and the chimneys of the Pigeon House, and the framing
circle of the road along the edge of the bay, Dun Laoghaire,
Blackrock, Sandymount Tower, Ringsend and the city; then
the other half circle, Fairview, Marino, Clontarf, Raheny,
Kilbarrack, Baldoyle, to the height of Howth Head.

1 'The Fair Hills of
Holy Ireland' is an
English translation
of 'Bánchnoic
Éireann Ó',
a poem/song
by the poet
Donnchadh Ruadh
Mac Conmara
(1715–1810).

Sandymount Strand and the chimneys of Poolbeg Generating Station (earlier known as the Pigeon House).

I couldn't really see Kilbarrack or Baldoyle, but it was only that I knew they were there. So many belonging to me lay buried in Kilbarrack, the healthiest graveyard in Ireland, they said, because it was so near the sea, and I thought I could see the tricolour waving over Dan Head's grave,[2] which I could not from ten miles over the bay. And I could see Baldoyle there, because it was the races.

'Passport, travel permit or identity document, please,' said the immigration man beside me. I handed him the expulsion order. He read it, looked at it and handed it back to me. He had a long educated countryman's sad face, like a teacher, and took my hand.

'Céad mile fáilte sa bhaile romhat.' A hundred thousand welcomes home to you.

I smiled and said, 'Go raibh maith agat.' Thanks.

He looked very serious, and tenderly enquired, 'Caithfidh go bhfuil sé go hiontach bheith saor.'

'Caithfidh go bhfuil.'

'It must be wonderful to be free.'

'It must,' said I, walked down the gangway, past a detective, and got on the train for Dublin.

2 Dan Head was a young IRA volunteer who died during the attack on the Custom House in May 1921.

Boozing with the Borstal Boy

The writer and sports journalist Bill Kelly (1922–96) grew up with Brendan Behan in Russell Street, Dublin. In the following extract from *Me Darlin'*

Brendan Behan, 1960.   *Dublin's Dead and Gone*, he gives an honest account of drinking with the writer and eventually distancing himself as Behan became more and more out of control. Behan had become a victim of his own success. The royalties he earned on his published works enabled him to drink more heavily until his creative ability was compromised.

From *Me Darlin' Dublin's Dead and Gone*

Boozing with the 'Borstal Boy' Brendan Behan, called for the thirst of a camel, the stamina of an ox, the stomach of an ostrich, and a neck like a jockey's buttocks. There are still people alive in Las Palmas, Paris, London, New York and Toronto who can testify to that statement. There are even some alive in Dublin, Behan's native city, who have survived the tidal wave of boisterousness and booze which was Behan on the bash. ...

I became involved with the ex-Borstal Boy through an innocent liking for the drink. I had known him as a kid when we lived near each other, but when his family moved out to the council-house suburb of Crumlin, I lost all trace of him, and didn't connect him with my childhood acquaintance when I saw the report in the newspaper that he and another man had been sentenced by a military court to imprisonment for shooting at a policeman after an IRA funeral. ...

Years later, John Ross, the thriller writer, invited me to a party in the Catacombs. The Catacombs was a peculiar semi-subterranean warren of rooms in Fitzwilliam Street, which was occupied at different times by various artists, writers, painters, and what have you. So far as I could figure, this party was being given by the Hon. John ffrench.[3]

Only for the fondness for drink that was on me, I wouldn't have gone, for I guessed I'd be out of place. I was, too, for the company was arty. There were artists, writers, sculptors, musicians, dancers – even a journalist or two. Perhaps by a very loose interpretation of the word I may have qualified for this latter category, as I had just sold two articles to the *Evening Herald* for two guineas each. I discovered later that I was no more phoney than most of them there, for as invariably happened in Ireland, the wish was taken for the deed, and most of the writers didn't write, the sculptors didn't sculpt and the artists didn't paint. I don't know about dancers or musicians – they didn't prove or disprove their claims, they just drank and talked.

3　John ffrench was an Irish ceramic artist.

All was going well in a haze of booze, cigarette smoke and noise, when the door burst open and there were men-and-women-girlish cries of 'It's Brendan,' over which rasped the coarse hoarse tones of your man: 'Givvus a drink for jaysake.'

The jacket was flying open, the shirt unbuttoned to the navel, the pants held up by a necktie, the hair was standing wild on the Nero-esque head as Behan followed his outthrust belly, in the wake of his full vocabulary, over to the bar.

The alleged Russian spy said to her girlfriend: 'That's Brendan Behan, he's delightfully coarse, don't you think?' and the friend concurred: 'Ooh yes, chahmingly gross.'

But Behan had no time for small talk. Straight from the door he headed, over to the well-stocked bar, a trestle set in the corner. He poured himself a drink, ignored the three or four people who crowded chattering around him, and fixed his bleary gaze on me. I didn't recognise him, after all the years, and his unwinking stare unnerved me slightly, for I feared he was going to denounce me as an interloper.

Then he bellowed: 'Hey Kelly. Come over here and have an effin drink for jaysake.' I went. He told me he remembered me from Russell Street, poured me a drink and made an announcement to the company.

'Now lissen all yis,' he said. 'I'm Brendan effin Behan, or if yis want to be nice, effing Brendan Behing, an me and me pal, Kelly here are goin' to drink. Any of yis that wants a drink, effin get it yourself.'

So Brendan Behing and I settled down to the serious business of getting sizzled, me half terrified of this wild-looking character who bore no resemblance to the skinny snotty kid I had known nearly twenty years earlier. So completely had I lost track of him that I didn't know he had been sent to Borstal for carrying explosives into Britain, or that he had been interned in the Curragh as an IRA man.

Had I known, I would have been terrified, but since I didn't and the booze was free and flowing, I settled in with him. ...

He went on talking, hopping from one subject to another – the Aran Islands, the tenements in Dublin, snatches of Gaelic, a bar of a song. He talked of painting – house painting – 'I'm a painter, you know, just like effin Hitler, but I'm not startin' any wars, I've had enough.' And he kept on talking, until between the drinks and the splatter of words and subjects, I drifted into an alcoholic euphoria. Brendan's face swelled and shrank, swayed and faded, appeared and disappeared, but the barrage of words kept battering against my ears, no longer intelligible to me, but somehow hypnotic, in a hoarse beery voice with the slight stammer that got worse as he got excited. Mechanically I kept on drinking. It seemed to me that the drink was having no effect on Behan, though looking back on it he must have been getting crocked, too.

How it ended, I don't know. About 2 a.m. I staggered out through the door and into the dark street. Nobody missed me. Nobody came to see if I was alright. So far as I know, Brendan Behan was still knocking them back. I know I got home, for I found myself in my own bed next day with the father and mother of all hangovers. ...

The Hostage, The Quare Fellow, Borstal Boy, Brendan Behan's New York – they were all in the future, lurking somewhere at the back of Behan's massive head.

I was doing a minimum amount of work which left me with a maximum of time, and Brendan was writing casual articles for the *Irish Press* – little gems they turned out to be – and the combination was dangerous. We met three or four times a week for drinking purposes, and invariably ended up doing the Stations of the Cross, as Behan called it, crawling from pub to pub. We were never really too broke to drink. If I hadn't a friend I could tap, Brendan had.

Looking gloomily into the dregs of our glasses in the Palace[4] with no sign of relief forces arriving, Behan would suddenly burst out, 'Ah, eff this. Come on, there's a fella up in Neary's who'll give us a pound.' And there always was. People were always glad to help him out. ... Yet even armed with money, we couldn't make straight for the nearest bar.

4 The Palace Bar is a famous pub in Fleet Street, Dublin.

The Palace Bar, Fleet
Street.

Westmoreland Street.

5 Mountjoy Prison.

'I'm barred there – and there – that hungry effer barred
me last week for singin'. He's so miserable that if he owned
Switzerland he wouldn't give you a slide.' ... Behan, too,
was getting restless. He'd drag me from one bar to another
for no reason, and we'd abandon that after a short time for
yet another. 'Doin' the stations,' he'd grin, baring all the
two teeth in the front of his mouth. ...

But I was as much a Peter as the
rest. Some time later, I was waiting for
my date in Westmoreland Street, when
even the roar of the traffic in that busy
thoroughfare couldn't drown the roars
of Behan from the far side of the street.
'Hey, for jaysake, Bill, wait for me. Don't
get the effin bus. Wait.' Brendan, waving
a walking stick and hobbling across the
street, stopping or dodging the speeding
traffic, caught me before I could flee.

'Look, for jaysake,' he bellowed at the top of his voice,
'Sean Kavanagh's walking stick. I broke me effin ankle in
the 'Joy,⁵ and the dacent oul fella lent me his own stick.
I should have given it back to him when I got out, but I

still have it.' Brendan had been lodged in Mountjoy Prison after an altercation with the police, and Sean Kavanagh, the governor, lent him the walking stick. Incidentally, he never gave it back.

'I'm after bein' over at the *Press* and up in your place and over in the *Times*, trying to get some bleedin' money off them and I can't get it,' he bellowed. 'Come on and buy us an effin drink'. ...

I cringed, afraid my date would come along, and the good impression I had carefully fostered would be shattered. As rapidly as I could, I whisked him round the corner into the Palace, bought two pints, gave him five shillings, finished my drink, and muttering something, dashed off, ten minutes late for my date but with my façade of respectability intact.

A week later, coming from the cinema with the same girl, I saw a commotion starting at a political meeting at the corner of Abbey Street, and heard Behan's stentorian profanity rising above the jumble of noise. Doing a rapid about-face, I wheeled her across the street and home.

My third betrayal came a few weeks later, on a Saturday night. I was working in the *Sunday Press*, and on 'cutline'[6] was going for a drink in the Scotch House. One of the reporters stopped me: 'Behan's up there at the corner of Hawkins Street, maggoty drunk, fighting with a policeman.' And I turned on my heel and went round to Mulligans, cursing myself for a coward, for I might possibly have got him away from the policeman quietly. If I had I would have saved him an appearance in court. ...

The last time I saw him was shortly before he died. He was in Tommy Moore's in Cathedral Street with another man, a stranger to me. Behan was standing at the counter, shirt and pants pulled over his pyjamas, the bug wild-haired head of him canted to one side, the eyes dull and unseeing.

I called hello to him and he slurred, 'Who the effin hell are you?' Then as I came closer, he recognised me. 'Ah Bill, how are yeh? Have an effin drink. I ran out of

6 Writing captions for photos.

the hospital for a jar – I couldn't stick it any more.' But I refused, had my own drink and went out.

I could see death in him, and he refusing to accept it, as if he believed that by standing in a bar as he had done so many times, he could keep the reaper at bay.

It was a funny kind of parting from me 'oul china,'[7] the Borstal Boy who had grown up to be a patriot, a gunman, a playwright, a writer and one of Dublin's characters, a fellow about whom more legends have grown up since he died than about Finn McCoole himself.

He died in March 1964. The world and his mother were at the funeral. The people who had run out of bars when he arrived were there, talking, telling of their intimacy with Brendan, the genius of him that they had recognised under all the coarseness and profanity for which they had forgiven him because he was a genius.

They boasted at the funeral, too, about their times with him, the Peters who didn't want to know him before he became famous, and who avoided him when he was drunk, which was often, or when he was broke, which was often too. They were safe now. Brendan Behing was dead. ...

They were at the graveside too, his friends, the oul wans, the cabbies, the dockers, and the few genuine friends he had in literary Dublin.

I didn't go to Glasnevin. I knew there'd be enough there without me. Instead I went into Tommy Moore's pub and had 'an effin pint for jaysake.' My boozing with the Borstal Boy was irrevocably finished.

7   Cockney rhyming slang for 'mate'. 'China plate': mate.

Dublin Banter: House Painter

I wrote the following poem for a show the former SIPTU president and trade union activist Des Geraghty staged in the Liberty Hall Theatre in May 2012 as part of the Larkin Hedge School programme. Entitled 'Brendan Behan, An Buachaill Caoin' ('Brendan Behan, the Gentle Boy'), it celebrated Behan's life. The poem was originally written in Irish, but I include the English translation here.

Brendan

(*A tribute to Brendan Behan*)

Glasnevin Cemetery.

Your talk, larger than Borstal or Mountjoy,
defined your world: saw you ejected
from hotels and pubs as you sang loudly

of smiling boys and Republican splits,
the bravado of your legend on stage
and in print, the collars of frothing pints

tracing your upper lip, your expletives
firing each sentence like gelignite or
scandalising smartly tweeded ladies.

Your battle, no longer against the Crown,
was waged against a bottle, your resolve
trembling, like a penny candle, between

Brendan Behan by
John Coll, Royal
Canal.

the artist within and the cruel demon
without, until your vision grew dim and
your words failed you as you lapsed all too soon

into your final stupor and left us;
your legacy enduring wherever
Dublin banter primes among house painters.

CHAPTER 13

Libertines

The Liberties, that area of inner-city Dublin generally within the catchment area of St Patrick's and Christchurch cathedrals, has been the birthplace of many famous Dubliners over the years. From James Clarence Mangan to Zozimus, the late Brendan Grace and Imelda May, the area enjoys a rich history stretching back to medieval times. My own father, Matthew Collinge, came from Malpas Street, while my grandparents lived in the Iveagh Buildings before their deaths. Despite recession and urban decay, the Liberties of Dublin still retains that essential spirit of the city – especially in its colourful inhabitants.

Mark Jenkins

Mark Jenkins is a local historian living in the Liberties. He leads general and themed walking tours of the area, regularly and on occasions such as Culture Night and Heritage Week. He has written tour scripts for St Patrick's Festival and won a flash fiction award for a piece he wrote on Tommy 'Liberty Boy' Lee from the area. Mark has worked in the James Joyce Library since 1998. Here he describes his neighbourhood, the Liberties of Dublin.

The Liberties towards the city centre.

The Liberties of Dublin

The Liberties of Dublin have long been regarded as the historic heart of Dublin. Over centuries the area has been known for its colourful characters, industries and lively street traders. ...

The area popularly known as the Liberties comprises what were the immediate boundaries of three liberties: the liberty of the abbey of St Thomas and Donore, the liberty of St Patrick's, and the liberty of St Sepulchre. They were often afforded rights such as the exemption from city taxes and were allowed privileges ranging from the right to brew their own beer (mead) and claim rents from many manors, carucates of land[1] and arable areas gifted to them. They had their own courts and prisons, presided over by a seneschal.[2]

One of the most important establishments in the area was the foundation of the abbey of St Thomas the Martyr in 1177. After the killing of Thomas á Becket at Canterbury Cathedral and his subsequent canonization, King Henry II promised to set up religious foundations around Europe in honour of the saint. It is from this abbey that the western highway along the historic Sligh Mhór, Thomas Street, gets its name. The abbey was bestowed tracts of land in Dublin, Bray, Co. Wicklow, and many other counties. As

1   A carucate is 120 acres.

2   Governor.

a result, the abbey was a very wealthy foundation and the source of much jealousy and many disputes in regard to its rights. The charters establishing the various rights were often referred to if required. The abbey enjoyed its status until the dissolution of the monasteries by Henry VIII when it was repossessed, and its lands given to Sir William Brabazon. ...

Successive generations of Brabazons were associated with the development of the liberties and were responsible for many benevolent endeavours in the area. The Earls of Meath were responsible for the establishment of the Meath and Coombe hospitals and the Meath Loan Company, which helped the poor of the area. They were also involved in later initiatives like the Artisan Dwellings Company to provide affordable housing. Many street names are linked back to the family such as Earl Street, Meath Street, Brabazon Street, Reginald Street, etc. The Brabazon family are still to be found at what became their family seat at Kilruddery House, near Bray.

Recent archaeological digs at the site of the abbey of St Thomas, on the famous old Frawley's store site, revealed bodies buried with scallop shells, a symbol of religious pilgrimage. For centuries citizens of the area have made their way along the route of the Camino de Santiago from the traditional starting point of the church of St James. Many returned with these shells as memorabilia.

The Liberty of St Patrick consisted of a small network of congested alleys and streets in the immediate vicinity of the cathedral. Many noted names lived in the area over time. The songwriter P.J. McCall, who wrote the famous ballads *Boolavogue* and *Follow me up to Carlow* and his *Irish Fireside Songs*, was born on Patrick Street at number 25 where his father was a successful publican. On Bride Street lived the nationalist poet James Clarence Mangan (*My Dark Rosaleen*, etc.). The most prominent and famous resident, however, was the famous author and dean of the cathedral Jonathan Swift. Gaining early fame and notoriety initially under a pseudonym, he was popular for such works as the *Drapier's Letters*, *A Tale of a*

Tub, *A Modest Proposal* and his timeless satire, *Gulliver's Travels*.

The Liberty of St Sepulchre was the domain of the Archbishop of Dublin, with its centre at the former palace on Kevin Street, subsequently a barracks and Garda station. It too had its own prison and court, even erecting a gallows at the outer boundary at Harold's Cross to warn people that they were entering the liberty. ...

Weaver's Hall.

A curious old tradition related to the boundaries of each liberty was known as 'the riding of the franchises'. Many trade guilds were based in the liberties outside the city walls and in meeting houses and halls, such as Tailor's Hall and Weaver's in the Coombe. Each liberty would have their day of extravagant displays and pageants along their boundaries. Seneschals were fined if they did not attend. The parades often attracted people from abroad to view the vibrant exhibitions and trades at work on elaborate carts. The Lord Mayor would also ride the fringes of his jurisdiction; one remnant that still survives is when a new lord mayor casts a spear into the sea symbolically, to define how far the boundary of his jurisdiction extends. The riding of the franchises continued until the Liberties were eventually absorbed back into the city and divided into wards.

The Liberties has always been noted for its industries, most notably textiles, brewing and distilling. A prolific period in the seventeenth century led to significant development and influx in numbers. A statute designed to attract artisans to Ireland, 'An act for encouraging Protestant strangers and others, to inhabit and plant in Ireland', saw many enticed to the area. Further to this, after the revocation of the Edict of Nantes, many French and Dutch

Huguenots fleeing religious persecution moved to the Liberties. They brought skills in textiles, weaving and poplin making to the area and the building of 'Dutch Billy' styled housing, giving employment to many. The gabled roofing enabled the use of looms in the upper floors of the houses, many being dotted around Mill Street, Weaver Square, Pimlico and Marrowbone Lane.

The products garnered international reputation but would decline due to harsh taxation at the request of English weavers. The hardship endured during wet winters, preventing the drying of cloths, led to the philanthropist Thomas Pleasants paying for the construction of the stove tenterhouse on Cork St/Brickfield Lane, where they could dry the materials stretched on tenterhooks.

The eighteenth century saw the rise of brewing and distilling businesses that are still famous. From humble beginnings, renting from Mark Rainsford, Arthur Guinness established the brand that would become, at one stage, the biggest brewery in the world. By 1798 one in two addresses on Thomas Street were licensed to sell spirits: Sweetman's, Watkins, Phoenix and Manders, to name but a few, were successful brewing operations. Again, with modest premises on Thomas Street, John Power began producing his brand and was one of the first to bottle whiskey, which had previously been sold by hogshead. The Liberties was the location for what became known as the 'Golden Triangle' as the whiskey business (William Jameson, George Roe & Co, Powers) flourished and demand increased. A combination of taxes, black market spirits, the quicker production of Scottish whisky and the rise of the temperance movement, meant a decline in their fortunes and, in some cases, closure.

Today sees a rebirth of whiskey in the Liberties: Teeling Whiskey opened on the site of Newmarket which was developed in 1674 by the Earl of Meath. Pearse Lyons Distillery operates in the converted church of St James. The Roe & Co brand has been revived at the site of the old Guinness powerhouse, and the Dublin Liberties Distillery on the site of an old mill and tannery on Mill Street.

Teeling Whiskey
Distillery.

In addition to its larger industries, the region has always been known for its vibrant street traders and associated characters, storytellers, and balladeers over the centuries. The Municipal Corporation once tried to ban hawkers on prominent areas like Thomas Street and Meath Street by declaring that nobody could lay down their wares on the footpaths anymore. The traders responded by wearing baskets around their necks and, soon after, business resumed as usual!

The Liberties, in previous years, was known as the area that the Celtic Tiger forgot. In recent years, small-and-large-scale project developments, both public and private, have seen some successes. The first playgrounds in Dublin were in Pimlico and New Row South in 1887, opened by the Lord Lieutenant and Marchioness of Derry (paid for by Lord and Lady Meath). More recently, the first playground in the area in a hundred years was opened at Weaver Park. The conservation of 10 Mill Street, the re-use of St Luke's church and sensitive conversion at St James's have all been well received, with the result that the Liberties is proving an increasingly desirable place to live and work. Archaeological works on foot of some of the redevelopments, continue to reveal a great deal about the rich history of this unique and wonderful area of Dublin.

Gerard Smyth

Liberties-born Gerard Smyth is an award-winning poet who has read his poetry internationally from Moscow to Minneapolis and has been poetry editor of the *Irish Times*. His poems have been widely translated. The following poem describes passing his former school, Carman's Hall, in Dublin's Spitalfields – an occasion which brings to mind harsh days of corporal punishment.

A School

I hear a school bell every time
I pass through *Carman's Hall*,
feel the hand that woke me from my trance,
hear again the questions asked,
the morning roll-call droning on.
This was where each day we saw a new word chalked
    in white,
pictures we drew were never of real life.
The high-walled yard is quiet
without the din of playtime voices
breaking into shouts and shrieks:
the trickster who meant no harm,
the brute who did
and liked to leave a mark on skin.
This was where we declared our wars,
set out on campaigns in our battleships,
mimed what we saw in gangster films –
before going inside to drink school milk,
face the punishment for mistakes,
the sharp command *Hold out your hands*.

Down by Christchurch

The Dublin song 'Easy and Slow', whose origin is unknown, has been attributed both to Sean O'Casey and Dominic Behan, the latter claiming he heard it from a female friend.

Christchurch
Cathedral.

Easy and Slow

It was down by Christchurch that I first met
    with Annie
A neat little girl and not a bit shy,
She told me her father who came from
    Dungannon,
Would take her back home in the sweet bye
    and bye.

And what's that to any man, whether or no,
Whether I'm easy, or whether I'm true,
As I lifted her petticoat, easy and slow
And I tied up my sleeve for to buckle her shoe.

All along Thomas Street down to the Liffey
The sunlight was gone, and the evening grew
    dark,
Along by King's Bridge and by God in a jiffy,
My arms were around her, beyond in the park.

And what's that to any man, whether or no,
Whether I'm easy, or whether I'm true,
As I lifted her petticoat, easy and slow
And I tied up my sleeve for to buckle her shoe.

Oh, from city or country, a girl is a jewel
And well made for grippin', as most of them
    are,
But any young fellow is really a fool
If he tries at the first time to go a bit far.

And what's that to any man, whether or no,
Whether I'm easy, or whether I'm true,
As I lifted her petticoat, easy and slow
And I tied up my sleeve for to buckle her shoe.
And if ever you go, to the town of Dungannon
You can search till your eyeballs are empty and
    blind,
Be you lyin' or walkin' or sittin' or runnin'
A girl like Annie you never will find.

And what's that to any man, whether or no,
Whether I'm easy, or whether I'm true,
As I lifted her petticoat, easy and slow
And I tied up my sleeve for to buckle her shoe.

James Lawless

James Lawless is an award-winning poet and author who was born in the Liberties. His most recent novel, *Letters to Jude*, has been acclaimed as Joycean in its scope and content.

James's mother, Catherine Lawless (*neé* Geraghty), came from the Liberties and the following poem movingly describes the sheer physicality involved for young mothers with children in prams to ascend the steps of the many storeys in the buildings where there were no lifts. Young James struggled to help his mother carry the pram up the steps.

Ascending a Liberties Stairway in 1952
Slate-grey steps with white ribbed bone to steady the
     foot
with the marks of the washerwoman's knees
and a black iron snake to hold on to
as it coiled its way upwards,
polished smooth from the caress of hands;
and the concrete landing
where we stopped to catch our breath
and a glimpse of the stars
through a rectangular opening in an ash-grey wall
which to its side housed a handled steel door,
a chute to the Great Bin
at the bottom of the stairs,
locked in a room of its very own
where it could overflow to its heart's content
and still take more,
the extractor of all the Liberties' ills;
and the automatic light
suddenly quenched itself on the landing
– we were overstaying our time
watching the stars twinkle –
and my baby sister cried from the darkness

as we continued our ascent.
I helped my mother tilt and lift;
I could hear her heavy breathing,
each slow tortuous step its own individual,
our very own little Calvary.
The baby cried again:
'Hush now, we're nearly there, alanna,' said Mam,[3]
but we were only halfway up with the pram.

3 Alanna: from the
Irish *a leanbh* (my
child).

Catherine Foley

Catherine Foley is an award-winning author, journalist and essayist. A regular contributor to the radio programme *Sunday Miscellany*, she is a fluent Irish speaker and has made a number of documentaries. In the following extract from her memoir *Beyond the Breakwater* (2018) Catherine describes moving into a house in the Liberties of Dublin and immediately sensing the presence of inner-city people who formerly inhabited the building.

My Street

There were three rowan trees across from my house in the Liberties in Dublin. My mother said these trees were lucky. They bore red berries in the autumn and their frayed leaves, which were like yellow hands, were bony and long-fingered. In the summer the leaves turned a darker green.

Sometimes I saw little boys running under the branches but that didn't happen too often because the trees were off-limits, really, standing in a narrow space behind railings that front a block of flats. This was a nicely proportioned four-storey block that was art-deco in design as a knowledgeable architect friend once told me. I swelled with pride the day he told me and we both looked across at my new inner city neighbours and enjoyed the straight lines that curved stylishly at the top around the windows and corners, the ridged divisions between the storeys and the newly cleaned red sandstone brickwork.

On another day, my next-door neighbour told me that our street ran along good ley lines, which are ancient straight 'paths' or routes in the landscape that are believed to have spiritual significance. I felt immediately that she was right. All the signs for a fair sailing in my new home were good.

The street was in the city centre, located near a busy junction where the cars whizzed by. Some of my neighbours had lived here all their lives. Occasionally they sat on their front steps and took the sun, hidden behind the parked cars. Sometimes they stood chatting in their doorways and watched the world go by when the evening came in.

At night I heard the couples and friends going home from the pub – singing, shouting, cursing, roaring, contradicting each other, and I smiled at the stories that were unfolding underneath my window. I imagined I was living in Pigalle, the red-light district of Paris, when there were fierce fights below and I sometimes wondered if I would find a body lying in a pool of blood on the footpath the next day. But the voices usually faded and they passed along up the street, making their way home. Their anger died out gradually and, as it got later and quieter, all I heard were the cars swishing by, and once the

Luas tram stop outside St James's Hospital.

Luas[4] had been built, I'd hear the driver ringing the bell as he motored towards the stop at St James's Hospital. It used to sound like a special goodnight salute to me and to all of us in our beds listening to the night – *ding, ding*, he seemed to say. *Ding, ding!*

4   A tram/light rail service introduced in 2004.

I often think of the family that grew up in my house before I lived here. When I first got the key, I walked through the rooms gingerly in case I disturbed anyone – even though I knew it was empty. Still, I jumped when I saw the walking stick and the plastic Christmas tree lying in the corner of the old wardrobe upstairs. For a moment, it was as if I had intruded on someone else's time and space.

Voices echo through a house, words reverberate on a stairway, on a landing; sounds of pots and pans in a kitchen must surely leave an imprint. I wonder is there a way of recapturing those incidental noises – of children talking, of parents whispering, of visitors laughing – and replaying them. Do sounds of a family remain in the space to be discovered, to be replayed? Sometimes in the evening when I came in, I found myself saying hello to the empty hallway – half in response to a feeling that the house had been waiting in silence for me to return and half in response to the sounds that had once filled its rooms.

I think that's why I love Walter de la Mare's poem, *The Listeners*:

'Is there anybody there?' said the Traveller
Knocking on the moonlit door; ...
And he smote upon the door again a second time;
'Is there anybody there?' he said.
But no one descended to the Traveller.

Of course, I'd have jumped out of my skin if anyone had 'descended to me' in my house. Thankfully it was the same for me as it was for the traveller:

No head from the leaf-fringed sill
Leaned over and looked into his grey eyes,
Where he stood perplexed and still.

However, as in the poem, there was a sense in my new place that there was another level of sound, another level of presence, that there was 'a host of phantom listeners that dwelt in the lone house then,' who were witness to me as they had been to the traveller:

Ay, they heard his foot upon the stirrup,
And the sound of iron on stone.

When I first moved in I set about stripping the walls. There were several layers of wallpaper in each room – I peeled each strip away and I got a glimpse of the other eras, like the times when yellow roses were the ultimate in chic or a lilac flock motif was chosen by the woman of the house for the master bedroom. There was a pink horizontal print too, and brown and orange circles that I'm sure must have dated from the 1970s. It seemed as if a family's history was there, waiting to be understood. There were light fittings and finishes that were evidence of forgotten styles from the 1960s and even earlier.

I knew that the elderly man who had lived in the house before I moved in had reared his family here. I imagined him and his wife as they were when they'd moved in first as a young couple. It must have been back in the 1940s.

After stripping another layer in the small bedroom, I discovered that they, the previous owners, had, at some point, decided to paper and decorate the room in a deep mauve colour. I wondered what year they'd decided to do this and at what point in their lives they'd been. They must have chosen the paper and matched it with a certain colour of paint, with light fittings and a style of carpet or linoleum for the floor. I hoped they were happy and I'm sure they were – one or two of the neighbours mentioned them to me, and I also felt they were happy because the house, in its stillness, possessed a pleasant calm.

Yes, the more I thought about it, I came to believe that a family's memories could linger in a space, that their voices only need to be tuned into, in order to be heard. I wondered if I would leave my memories behind too, to settle in corners, to resonate from the bricks.

Time slipped away, of course, and I am no longer living in that house. When it's empty again will the 'silence surge softly backwards,' as Walter de la Mare puts it? Even if I'd liked to leave an imprint – a sense of my time in that house, a sense perhaps that I was in tune with the vibrations – I suppose, in the end, all you will hear is the silence.

Rambling Houses

In 2011 the renowned traditional musician Tony McMahon had a 'rambling house' (a house where

John Dillon Street in Dublin's Liberties.

people gathered to talk, play cards or listen to music and fireside tales) in the Liberties with excellent traditional music, poetry and chat. Tony was convinced that there were echoes in his house of those generations that had gone before, good people who had lived modest lives without recognition. 'Port na bPúcaí', or 'Music of the Spirits', is a slow traditional air, reputedly picked up by a fisherman on the Blasket Islands who heard the fairies playing. I wrote the following poem as a tribute to Tony, to the music and to the ordinary people of the inner city. Though originally written in Irish, I include the English translation here. Tony passed away in October 2021 and I was honoured to read this poem at his funeral service.

Music of the Spirits
(*For Tony McMahon*)

5   The Siege of Ennis is a traditional céilí dance, usually involving eight dancers.

After the Siege of Ennis[5] in the Liberties,
we thronged into the small inner city house
to experience Otherworld music.

For a short while we no longer heard the jingle
of radio, television or mobile phone, merely the ripple
of fairy music, once wafted by the breeze
on a moonlit island, its grace notes
captured by a startled fiddler,
its phrases still troubling his soul –

From the walls of the old house towards us
crept the shades of working people from the Square,
labourers and tradesmen in their working clothes,

housewives with their ragged children
in bare feet, young darlings in their petticoats,
all enticed by the enchanted box music,

until the house itself became an instrument
from which clear notes were wrung:
pride of race, life and death, passion, solitude.

I defer to the musician, to the music,
to the shades of the small house, to night visits of
	old,
and I can still hear spirit music in my sleep.

CHAPTER 14

Swinging Dublin – The 1960s

While the 1960s in Britain heralded great social change, from the Profumo scandal to 'Beatlemania' to Mods and Rockers, change was slower in Dublin, and especially outside the city in rural areas. De Valera's idyll of 'athletic youths and happy maidens' was being challenged by young Dubliners, nevertheless, who now had access to jobs and a degree of wealth never experienced by their parents after the success of Seán Lemass's First Programme for Economic Expansion. Hair styles and clothing mirrored their English

O'Connell Street, 1963. Reproduced courtesy of the National Library of Ireland.

The Dubliners, 1970s.

counterparts, and a growing resentment against strict authority and religious mores saw a youth culture develop in the city that preferred beat music to traditional Irish music and even that of the showbands. The 'ballad boom' of the 1960s encouraged young people to throng to beer festivals around the country where a tent, a groundsheet and a few six-packs of beer meant unbridled freedom away from concerned parents. JFK's visit to Dublin further underscored the cult of youth, as the young president's boyish good looks contrasted with those of Irish politicians – many of whom were veterans of the War of Independence.

The Dubliners

Formed originally in 1962, as an offshoot of the Ronnie Drew Ballad Group, by 1964 the Dubliners comprised the following musicians: Ronnie Drew on Spanish guitar and vocals, Luke Kelly on banjo and vocals, Barney McKenna on tenor banjo, John Sheahan on fiddle and Ciarán Bourke on guitar, tin whistle, harmonica and vocals. The group went on to enjoy international fame, although they were never quite as successful as the Clancy Brothers in America. Luke Kelly, who had a powerful voice, was a fine interpreter of ballads over the years, while Ronnie Drew's deep, gravelly voice was an inimitable second. Over a period of fifty years the Dubliners' line-up changed, with such musicians as Bobby Lynch, Jim McCann, Paddy Reilly, Seán Campbell and Paddy Watchorn joining the group. The Dubliners released over thirty studio albums and were loved in Ireland, especially during the ballad boom, when the atmosphere was electric at their concerts with the audience singing along. Musical 'jousting' between John Sheahan on fiddle and Barney McKenna on tenor banjo was a tour de force. The Dubliners also managed to get into the British top ten, appearing on *Top of the Pops*. Fiddler John Sheahan is the only surviving member of the original group.

The following poem, from my collection *Fearful Symmetry*, describes a famous concert in the Embankment pub outside Tallaght in Dublin, when my young friends and I thrilled to the music of the Dubliners. Since they sang 'The Monto' that night, about a famous red-light area in Dublin, I used imagery from the Circe episode of James Joyce's *Ulysses*, which is also set in this infamous district. Joyce refers to it as 'Nighttown'.

Dubliners Concert 1966

Our eyes are dazed from Celebration[1]
our minds too full to think,
serried tankards line the table:
Guinness, Double Diamond,
(The beer the men drink).[2]

We welcome our idol
with rowdy delight,
Luke Kelly cheered onto the stage,
craggy in fiendish goatee,
haloed by the spotlight
in blasphemous parody,
loudly singing 'The Monto,'
making our night.

Rainbow fans and gaping doors
loom before our bloodshot eyes,
Nighttown and its whores
brazen, Mabbot streetwise,[3]
loiterers and gaffers
from the Gloucester
Diamond, raucous humour –

Too young to know the lure
of gaudy dollwomen, we are prey
to comely maidens of the day:
Enchantresses in hipster skirts
and Mary Quant eyes,

1 Celebration was a beer brewed by Guinness in 1966.

2 'Double Diamond, the beer the men drink' is a quote from an advertisement for Watney's keg beer at that time.

3 Mabbot Street marked the entrance to Nighttown/the Monto.

bluer than blue,
swinging to the chorus of the times,
'Take her up to Monto,
Langeroo to you!'

Luke Kelly's Funeral

The late Luke Kelly (1940–84) was one of Dublin's most famous singers. Born in Dublin's inner city, he emigrated to England in his late teens and there began to sing folk songs in the small clubs, to the accompaniment of his banjo. He was heavily influenced by the singer-songwriter Ewan MacColl and was a socialist activist on behalf of working people. On his return to Ireland in the early 1960s, he was caught up in the ballad boom. He joined the Dubliners and attained worldwide fame as an interpreter of ballad and folk songs. Luke died of a brain tumour in 1984. The following is a description of his funeral in the Church of the Holy Child, Whitehall, from Des Geraghty's book *Luke Kelly: A Memoir* (1994).

From *Luke Kelly: A Memoir*

John Sheahan organised the music for his funeral, with the assistance of John Curran, who wrote a special arrangement for trombones and trumpets of 'The Old Triangle.' The melody included the songs Luke was famous for, and some of his favourites, including a composition of John's called 'The Prodigal Son,' which Luke used to introduce on stage, John said, with 'ladies and gentlemen, Johann Sebastian Sheahan,' and a big grin on his face.

Barney McKenna and Luke's three brothers carried the coffin, covered in wreaths, including a bright red one tied with a green ribbon, with a simple inscription marking a friendship which went back to the days when the Dubliners were on their first tour of Germany. It said 'From Paul McCartney and Ringo Starr.'

The celebrities who crowded into the church in Whitehall for his funeral ranged from political leaders to soccer stars and every area of the performing arts. And though Luke may have felt it would be small-minded to approach God, there were half a dozen clergymen on the altar anxious to intercede on his behalf. I stayed outside the door with some of Luke's old friends, most of whom were never very prominent at the altar rails of any church.

But it was not the number of celebrities or priests that mattered; it was the plain people of Dublin, who considered Luke a personal friend. As Dick Grogan wrote of the removal in the *Irish Times*, 'Luke Kelly's people filled the Church of the Holy Child in Whitehall last night to keep a Dubliner company on the first stage of his final journey: ordinary people, workers, trade unionists, musicians, actors, friends. They thronged the vast, vaulted expanses of one of north Dublin's largest churches and spilled over into the car park outside. Hundreds of cars followed the cortège for the removal of the body from the Richmond Hospital through relentless rain ...'

Ronnie Drew noticed a couple of fellows working on the road outside who came into the church on their tea break to pay their respects and his brother was approached outside the church by a bewildered elderly man who gazed uncomprehendingly at the crowds and asked: 'Excuse me, son, is today a holy day or what?'

According to some, in the last months of his life Luke was most drawn to a song that had been a favourite of his for years, seldom sung but on his compilation album released in 1982. It was called 'The Unquiet Grave':

The wind that blows today, my love,
A few small drops of rain.
I never had but one true love
In cold clay she is lain ...

Afterword

On 30 January 2019, the thirty-fifth anniversary of Luke Kelly's death, two statues were unveiled in his memory: one on South King Street, by sculptor John Coll; the other on the north side of the city on

Guild Street, by artist Vera Klute. Family friend Des
Geraghty explained:

> One is on the Northside where
> Luke came from. It's right in the
> heart of the financial services area,
> but also an area where we have a
> lot of working-class people – poor
> over the years, and struggling for an
> existence. But [there's also one] on
> the other side of the city, where Luke
> would actually have frequented ...
> among the watering holes close
> to Grafton Street. He busked, he
> played, and was well known around
> that area.

Luke Kelly by Vera
Klute.

JFK

In June 1963 President John F. Kennedy visited
Ireland. There was great excitement throughout the
country with the fledgling Teilifís Éireann (now
RTÉ) covering its first major event since its inception
on 31 December 1961. Between 26 and 29 June, the
president visited Dublin, Wexford, Cork and Galway.
Before he left on Air Force One he promised that he
would return in the spring but his plans were cut short
tragically when he was assassinated on 22 November
1963.

The following extract from an article of mine,
first broadcast on *Sunday Miscellany* (RTÉ Radio) in
November 2018, recalls my own visit with my friend
the late Frank Murray to Westmoreland Street,
Dublin, to see the president.

Dublin Welcomes JFK

By late June of 1963, John Fitzgerald Kennedy landed in
Dublin fresh from visiting the Berlin Wall where he made
his famous speech 'Ich bin ein Berliner'. This was a magic
time with the handsome young president coming back

President John
F. Kennedy with
Taoiseach Seán
Lemass, American
Embassy, Dublin, 1963.

to his ancestral home. Ireland welcomed him as it would
royalty and the atmosphere was electric.

I was thirteen then. That afternoon, my friend Frank
Murray – who would go on, in later life, to a career in the
music business, managing the Pogues – called for me. He
said he was going into town 'to see President Kennedy'
and I secured my racing pigeons in their loft in my back
garden and headed off enthusiastically with him on the
50 bus. Both of us pushed our way to the front of the
huge crowd in Westmoreland Street and then there was
a palpable hush as the large open-top car came slowly
into view. Despite the presence of security men – easily
discernible by their crew-cuts and white trench coats –
the crowd surged forward and the young president,
tanned and resplendent in a light blue suit, reached out
and began shaking hands.

As he came close Frank called out, 'Welcome to
Dublin, President Kennedy,' to which JFK answered,
'Thanks, kid.' Then he shook our hands as women, young
and old, swooned around us. We heard one of them say,
'Isn't he only gorgeous. Wouldn't yez wish he'd faint and
I could give him de kiss o' death!' to which the crowd
erupted in laughter.

Frank and I returned home excitedly that day and
followed the next few days' events on TV as the pageant
of JFK continued, taking in Wexford and Limerick before
he departed on Air Force One from Shannon. That

final speech where he vowed to 'come back to see old Shannon's face again' was poignant even at the time; in retrospect it became heart-rendingly so.

On 22 November of that year, once more, it was my friend Frank Murray who knocked on our door to tell us that JFK had been assassinated in Dallas. I can still hear my sister's bitter crying and see my late mother's shocked white face. Fifty-five years on, as 22 November passes and I remember my friend, former Pogues manager Frank Murray, who passed away two years ago, I recall the glamour and warmth of those days despite the chill of the Cold War. Regardless of how history may judge John Fitzgerald Kennedy, thirty-fifth president of the United States, my memories of this unique man will always be cherished.

Richard Barnwall

Richard Barnwall grew up on a farm in north County Dublin. He trained and worked as an architect but, after retiring, spent his time travelling extensively around the world on his motorcycle. He broadcast the extract which follows on *Sunday Miscellany*. In it, Richard describes the long journey he made as a teenager in 1968 into the Dublin Markets. He lists many places and features, some of which remain and others which have disappeared as the city expanded over the years.

Memories of the Old North Road

I recently travelled the Old North Road from Smithfield to The Naul, passing the Boot Inn on a remnant of this ancient 'way' now slowly being absorbed by the westerly reach of Dublin Airport. This trip, in the spring of 2018, marked also the fiftieth anniversary of my first road-legal drive to the Dublin Markets from our farm in the Leas along this very road. In 1968, at the age of 16, I was elevated to the role of driver on our small Ferguson tractor; fondly referred to as the 'Grey Mare' in the Ireland of the '50s. The load was a trailer of a hundred hay bales destined for Dodd's

Smithfield Horse Fair, 2008.

of Smithfield. I was retracing the route of my forefathers who supplied vegetable and dairy produce to the Dublin Markets. My rig was not dissimilar to the horse and cart of eighteenth century journeymen.

In that spring of 1968 Ireland was on the cusp of great change. Seán Lemass had begun a new era of progress. My journey on that day, but only in hindsight mind you, was full of evidence of this change.

The hay had come from our land on Balcultry Lane and I set out from the Leas at 7 a.m. at the dawn of a cold spring morning. My father would follow later in the VW Beetle with a small trailer of cabbage. This was a coming-of-age moment for me, the eldest son, drawing a man's load to the Dublin markets. The journey I faced had the same challenges as for earlier travellers, comprising river crossings with sharp descents and ascents – hard work for horses and the underpowered Ferguson alike.

My first and immediate test was the Ward River crossing at Knocksedan Bridge. A careful choice of gearing was necessary going downhill through Killeek Cross and again climbing the steep incline past Victor Bewley's dairy farm.

It was a clean run along the walls of Ussher's Demesne, then owned by Dr Cross, and past Willie Keeling's recently constructed glasshouses to the Forest

Cross. We maintained a level traverse, as suited a road first used by horse teams, and passed the then derelict Tavern at Pickardstown before reaching the Boot Inn. Matt Weldon ran the Boot Inn amid a small village, with a shop run by the Maxwell sisters.

To the left of the road was Collinstown Airport, clear to view, with the iconic 'modern' terminal designed by Desmond Fitzgerald. Across the plateau of Collinstown we passed the farms of the Monks, Longs, Duffs and Byrnes, as I recall, all nowadays under a carpet of aircraft runways.

The next river crossing was the Santry River at the seventeenth-century Charter School, also originally a stage stop on the ancient road. This was the steepest descent on the journey with the load pushing black smoke from the struggling Ferguson. I should say in passing that the only 'braking' available to me was engine power. The drum brakes on the tractor were nominal and the trailer had none at all. Life was simpler then. There were no indicators, brake lights, horn or mirrors to worry about.

Uphill to Ballymun Cross at Santry Avenue was uneventful with 'the father' passing me with a toot of the horn. We passed St Pappin's Church and School where I had begun my education some decade earlier. Shortly after were the yellow gates of the Model Farm. In 1968 Professor Drew and his family were gone and the tower blocks were under construction by Cubitt Haden Sisk, or so the sign-board said.

No traffic to worry about on the slow descent down Mobhi Road to cross the river Tolka. Uphill to Crossguns Bridge with Hedigan's Brian Boru pub on the right. A number of 'early men' on bicycles attached themselves to the trailer on our climb to Doyle's Corner. Now down Constitution Hill towards the King's Inns to negotiate the tight right hand turn at 'Ging' Morgan's butcher onto North King Street. A short step to Smithfield and I duly queued up in front of Dodd's in a mix of horse and carts, vans and trucks and 'oul wans' with their vegetable barrows and prams.

I was handed a docket and dispatched to 'Mossy' Crimmin's cattle yard on Prussia Street and was soon joined by 'the father'. Himself and Mossy (of the club foot) talked themselves into a reverie while I unloaded our cargo. I had little awareness of the great changes to come as I joined the market throng for a mug of tay (tea) and a rasher sandwich on Mary's Lane before the journey home.

My late father, who was born in 1921, was alert to the pace of change in his eighty-five years. He once asked me if any previous man in a lifetime could have witnessed what he had from the age of the horse (in his youth) to the era of modern transport and communications ... with a man sent on a visit to the moon!

So my recent retrace of the road to the Leas was cause for reflection. The Luas North tramway now crosses the old road at Broadstone. Peter Hedigan, with whom I started school in St Pappin's sixty years ago, still holds sway in the Brian Boru. The Charter School remains on the Santry River on a lonely spur, cut off by the M50. The Boot Inn holds out as an isolated outpost in a deserted village. The Forest Cross remains with Keeling's Fruit Farm – the only tangible evidence of the market farming heritage of this area.

Victor Bewley moved his Jersey herds away to Co. Meath from the noise of the airport in the '70s but Aungier's derelict Knocksedan Inn still commands the Ward River crossing. My mother, in her ninety-second year, still holds court in the Leas and the farm is still there, worked by my brother. The Norman motte and bridge still stand at Cnoc Sí Dan and the Banshee still calls occasionally ... so 'the mother' says!

Nelson's Pillar

Nelson's Pillar was a large granite column built in memory of Horatio Nelson to celebrate the admiral's defeat of the French and Spanish navies at the Battle of Trafalgar in 1805. A statue of Nelson, sculpted by the Cork-born sculptor Thomas Kirk, capped the column. After its erection in 1809 it was opened to the public and generations of Dubliners climbed the 168 steps, for a small fee, to stand on the Doric abacus and look down on the city.

While nationalists were unhappy that a monument celebrating an English admiral should sit in the centre of O'Connell Street, most Dubliners simply saw it as a familiar landmark. Writers such as W.B. Yeats, James Joyce and Oliver St John Gogarty were happy to preserve the pillar on historic grounds.

There were unconfirmed reports that the rebels had made an unsuccessful attempt to blow up the pillar during the 1916 Rising, but others discounted this, since the column gave the insurgents good cover as they dashed across O'Connell Street during the fighting.

Nelson's Pillar, Sackville Street (O'Connell Street).

Fifty years on, in the early hours of 8 March 1966, the pillar was blown up by republican activists. Many windows were shattered in O'Connell Street but, miraculously, no one was injured. The explosion did not blow up the entire statue, so a week later the Irish army blew up the remnant of the column in a controlled explosion. Crowds gathered for this event and there was a festive atmosphere in the city that evening.

As expected, Dublin wit was at its best, with one man saying, 'I thought they'd wait until December to budget!' Nelson's head was stolen from the corporation lock-up and it later appeared on stage with the Dubliners as well as on Killiney Beach in a fashion photo shoot. It can now be seen in the Gilbert Room of Pearse Street Library in Dublin.

Two songs about the event appeared in the charts soon afterwards: 'Up Went Nelson in Old Dublin' by the Go Lucky Four reached number one in the charts, while the Dubliners sang 'Nelson's Farewell' on their album *Finnegan Wakes*.

The Spire.

The Spire

Over the years O'Connell Street declined and saw the proliferation of fast-food restaurants, bargain shops and anti-social behaviour. Commencing in 1999, the street layout was redesigned, with statues being cleaned, some trees being cut down and traffic being redirected to allow better pedestrian access. A new monument called the Spire of Dublin (also known as the Monument of Light) – designed by Ian Ritchie Architects and manufactured in Waterford – was erected in 2003 on the spot where Nelson's Pillar originally stood. Standing at a height of 120 metres, it consists of eight hollow stainless steel cone sections, three metres in diameter at the base, narrowing to an apex of fifteen centimetres.

The Spire was met with mixed reactions, some Dubliners being unimpressed, others generally indifferent. As usual, nicknames for the Spire were soon heard in Dublin: 'the Stiletto in the Ghetto' and 'the Stiffy in the Liffey' being some of the more common ones. As with Nelson's Pillar before, it now serves as a convenient location for friends and couples to arrange to meet in Dublin's city centre.

Catherine Ann Cullen

Drogheda-born Catherine Ann Cullen is an award-winning poet, children's author and songwriter. She is an IRC postdoctoral fellow at UCD/Poetry Ireland, researching Dublin's lost street poets. She was Poetry Ireland's inaugural Poet in Residence.

In her poem 'Spike City', the city's Spire becomes a symbol of 'defensive architecture' aimed at deterring homeless street sleepers.

Spike City

We've made a bed of nails for you
outside our head office
to discourage you
one more time.

Some days you challenge us –
we find ourselves stepping over
a ragged yogi balanced
on the concrete spines.

We call it defensive architecture
as though we were under attack
from the rough sleeping
that our studs will make rougher.

There's a spike in homelessness
but it won't pierce
the glass edifice
where we practise mindfulness every Tuesday
 lunchtime.

We look straight ahead while
a tentative sky stretches over O'Connell St
trying to make itself comfortable
on a giant spike.

Phil Lynott and Pauline Fayne

Phil Lynott (1949–86), who grew up in Crumlin, was initially the frontman in the Black Eagles, who played regularly in the Moeran Hall in Walkinstown, before becoming a world rock legend with Thin Lizzy. Inchicore historian and poet Michael O'Flanagan recorded historic footage, on cine camera, of Phil Lynott and his band in the mid-1960s.

Pauline Fayne grew up in Crumlin before moving to Tallaght, where she now lives. She has published six collections of poetry. The following poem by Pauline is a tribute both to the late Phil and to Michael.

Thin Lizzy, 1973.

Philo
(*For Michael O'Flanagan the cameraman*)

Giggling teens,
in 'budgie' jackets
trip hazard flares
and high wedge heels

We admired the daring
of the graffiti artist
who sprayed your name
along the village walls

Hoped to meet you
at the Star Cinema or Fusco's chipper,
swore the Black Eagles
would be famous soon.

Today I watched again that film
of you running past our house
chasing your dreams down Somerville Avenue[4]
and wished I had been in the garden

shyly waving among the wallflowers
as you flashed your brilliant smile
at the cameraman,
striding towards stardom.

4   Pauline Fayne
    lived on Somerville
    Avenue, where the
    cine footage was
    taken.

Teri Murray

Poet, award-winning dramatist, short story writer and children's author Teri Murray grew up in Crumlin and lived in Limerick until her death in 2017. She published four collections of poetry.

Also on the theme of suburban Dublin, Teri recalls amateur theatre and puppet shows which were staged in a garden on Captain's Road during her childhood. Here, art imitated the life of the families in the estate.

The Globe on Captain's Road
At the amphitheatre
in Waldron's back garden,
we balanced on an old plank,
sipped juice from melted ice pops,
munched Marietta biscuits.
We could have been in the Abbey Theatre
watching a performance
of O'Casey or Brecht.
The puppets on Paul Hanna's hands
projected sagas onto a sheet
flapping on the line,
Captain Boyle stumbling home
from Mooney's in the village
Mother Courage catching
the early bus to do
a bit of a cleaning job;

screamed at Missus Punch,
tears blotting her paper-maché face
to hide the baby under the bed
away from her husband's
unrelenting fists;
booed at the Garda
as he tried to stop women
tussling over a ball that flattened
antirrhinums and dented
the symmetry of a privet hedge –
Warrior, magician, maid and hag
all the archetypes were there;
impersonating the neighbours,
exposing the quirks in our society
at the amphitheatre
in Waldron's back garden.

On Guided Tours
The following poem from my collection *Fearful
Symmetry* describes how my teenage friends and I went
on 'guided tours' more for the perks that such tours

St Michan's Church.

could provide than from any real educational interest. The Crusader referred to in the final stanza was desecrated by vandals who broke into the vault of St Michan's in 2019, and the head was stolen but later retrieved. 'Summer in the City' is the name of a Lovin' Spoonful hit from 1966.

Summer in the City

Bored with the suburbs
we gladden to summer
in the city, on guided tours
pruning our budget tighter
by sampling old reliables –[5]

In Player Wills we suffer
the deafening noise and
convoluted guide talk
to walk
among endless coils
of Virginia tobacco
and exit into
the visitors' room, eagerly
clutching our spoils,
mild, medium and tipped,
then puffing and coughing
we wend our way
along the quays
towards maturity.
In a certain brewery
we hold our noses tightly
on the catwalks
above the polished vats
to arrive at the guest bar,
there by far
the wiser, we instantly
acquire a taste for the plain[6]
things in life, Confirmation pledges
profaned,[7]

5   Beer and cigarettes were usually increased in price during consecutive budgets and hence known as 'the old reliables'.

6   Here, 'plain' refers to plain porter (as in Flann O'Brien's 'A pint o' plain is your only man').

7   It was customary for Catholic children at their confirmation to promise not to drink alcohol until they were eighteen.

obsolete as sherbet and lemonade.
Last port of call
St Michan's with its
cobwebbed vault and penitent's chair,
no Vincent Price or Boris Karloff,

Our guide is drier
than its limestone walls –
we shake hands pruriently
with the Crusader[8]
who yawns from the tedium
of contact, doomed for all eternity
to a travesty of truth
to the nightmare of history[9]
and the bland indifference of youth.

8   While the mummy is described as 'the Crusader', it is more likely that the body was from the seventeenth century.

9   Joyce's *Ulysses*: 'History … is the nightmare from which I am trying to awake.'

Marie Gahan

Award-winning poet, journalist and fiction writer Marie Gahan has been internationally acclaimed for her writing. She has facilitated creative writing classes for adults over the years with great success.

In this essay she describes the early days of her marriage, when she moved from her house on Galtymore Road in the Dublin suburb of Drimnagh to the Greenhills area which, at that time, was still among fields. She also tells the poignant story of Michael 'Chicken' Cullen, an elderly man who refused to move from his cottage at Walkinstown Cross, despite pressure from Dublin County Council.

From Galtymore to Greenhills

I came from Galtymore. My friends lived in Sperrin, Comeragh, Slievenamon and Benbulben. In school, we realised that all our roads in Drimnagh bore the names of Irish mountain ranges. Like so many sons and daughters who had grown up around us, I married a neighbour's child and was lured to a nearby estate, nestling in the dip on the Greenhills Road, with a magnificent view of the Dublin Mountains. It boasted spanking new houses, with

Dublin City from the
Wicklow Way in the
Dublin Mountains.

a mortgage we could just about afford. The bus only took us to Walkinstown Cross, so we had quite a walk to our new home, situated at the furthest reaches of the site and bordered by lush green fields.

As a bride, I never felt lonely living in a new housing estate. How could I! I knew so many people living around us. Like a lot of our new neighbours, we had family living close by. I met girls from school at the local caravan where we shopped for groceries at inflated prices. But imagine my surprise to recognise my old dancing partners in the guise of some of my neighbours' husbands.

Just back from honeymoon and settling in, a chance meeting with one of them set the tone for the rest. A Johnston Mooney and O'Brien bread van was parked on James's Road. As I neared it, the brown shop-coated deliveryman was sliding out a board full of bread from the back. He turned round and I recognised Gerry. We had enjoyed many a good jiving session in Mourne Road Hall. His handsome face broke into a smile, and I learned that he had a wife and a new baby son and lived nearby. Now button-down by responsibility, his fancy shirts and winkle-picker shoes had disappeared.

The back door of the van flung open to the world, we stood talking and laughing about old times, the mouth-watering aroma of freshly baked bread wafting between us. On impulse, he thrust two crusty turnovers into my hands, before leaping into the driving seat and hooting his horn as he drove off. It was a mundane present, in keeping with my new marital status perhaps, but one inspired by a generosity of spirit that brought a smile to my face.

Whilst walking, gardening or at Sunday Mass, I spotted several more old dance partners with whom I had quickstepped or swung to the saxophone. John, the wild one, was more handsome now that his teenage acne had cleared up. Scrawny Brian had filled out and he was looking the better for it. I didn't recognise Peter without his DA[10] haircut! I could see that they were finding their feet as new fathers and their dancing days were done. Their Beatle jackets (bumfreezers we used to call them) had been replaced by 'respectable' clothes.

As time went on, we rubbed shoulders at residents' associations, parent-teacher meetings or chatted in the local pub, if we were lucky enough to have a baby-sitter on a Saturday night. Sometimes we managed to have a jive or a quickstep just for old time's sake at our local dinner dance, injecting a little frisson into our lives of domesticity.

Many of our neighbours had sisters or brothers living in the estate, far enough for privacy but near enough to call on when needed. I had a sister, Ann. Irish twins – born eleven months apart – we were inseparable. Living as close as we did, we became sisters, best friends and neighbours all rolled into one – always there for each other to confide in, listen, lend a hand or understand.

On Tuesdays we'd walk all the way to Mam's house, pushing our babies in the bouncy high prams that precluded public transport. Mini-skirted and stiletto-heeled, comfort was the last thing on our minds as we set off on our journey. It took an hour from my gate to Mam's, down towards the Walkinstown roundabout, past St Agnes's Church and through Crumlin village. We had the back broken of our journey by the time we reached Crumlin Road. Summer and winter, we went, dressed in flimsy minidresses when the sun shone; fun-fur coats and knee-high boots in the frost, a hot-water bottle tucked inside each pram to keep the babies warm,

10 Duck's arse, a hairstyle common among Teddy Boys in the 1950s. The hair was greased back into a line at the back of the head, which apparently resembled a duck's hindquarters.

laughing and chatting all the way, eliciting a few wolf-whistles from men on the remaining building sites en route, to finally arrive to the glorious smell of Mam's stew emanating from her front door. Happy days!

My husband Tom had a hand in the disappearance of the beautiful green fields around us. Like our neighbours, he was one of a new generation of tradesmen: bricklayers, carpenters, electricians, plasterers, plumbers, not afraid of hard work in order to reap the reward of the seventies' building boom. As I pegged out washing on the line, trowel in hand, he'd wave to me from a scaffolding in the field behind our house that would soon become Greenpark (estate). ...

Looking back on my first year in Greenhills, I can remember Michael ('Chicken') Cullen leaning on the half-door of his cottage at Walkinstown Cross, smoking his pipe. He was a local legend because he had held up 'progress' for twenty-one years by his very presence on the spot that Dublin County Council had earmarked for a roundabout to relieve pressure on the ever-increasing traffic in the area.

From 1950 to 1971, he refused to leave his family home of generations, despite the fact that major road development was going on all around him and he was virtually living on an island, surrounded by heavy traffic, for many years. Never married, his family owned the freehold of their little cottage and when the council made him an offer, he dug his heels in and refused to budge. No pressure was put on him for many years, yet he was a constant thorn in the council's side.

They offered to build him a brand new two-bedroomed bungalow, just yards from his cottage on Walkinstown Avenue, at a nominal rate of six old pence a week. This didn't satisfy Chicken. He wasn't giving up the freehold of his cottage. Rumour had it that a TD[11] offered to pay the sixpence a week for him, but Chicken flatly refused. An independent man, he wouldn't be beholden to anyone. The old neighbours understood how he felt. The new bungalow stood empty and

11 Teachta Dála, a member of the Irish government.

Construction cranes silhouetted at sunset in the Dublin sky.

waiting. The council could not meet his demand for a freehold house without creating a precedent. ...

This old man's plight elicited sympathy from everyone. He was doing what everyone else would like to do and never got the chance. It was a stand against the Establishment; one man's fight against faceless bureaucracy. ...

When Chicken finally vacated his home, he did so voluntarily. He left his cottage at 2 a.m. one morning. Head held high, he walked with a neighbour across the road to his new bungalow. As soon as he did so, the council moved in. The waiting bulldozer hit the gable wall with a mighty bang. The men worked right through the night. By 8 a.m. the cottage was reduced to a pile of rubble. It was the end of an era.

Chicken sat in his new home, sipping tea with his niece. He'd got what he wanted – a freehold house to leave to his relatives. Victory was sweet, but sentiment was strong. Through the window he could see the council at work. As he watched his old home crumble to the ground, Michael Cullen wept openly.

He lived in his new house from the age of 86 until his death at 95. Many people felt that an old part of Walkinstown went with him, an old way of life that has, sadly, not been replaced. Nowadays, if you use the Walkinstown roundabout, you might notice the pole sticking up in the middle of it. That is the original vent sewage pole that was attached to the gable end of Michael Cullen's cottage. As you gird yourself for the onslaught of traffic, you could be excused for wondering just what the roundabout has achieved!

Yet, this is the place I love. Its people are my people. Now that my children have found their own green hills and pastures new, the cycle of life goes on. ... Now and then I run into my old dancing partners – pillars of society now – taking time out from the Credit Union or the junior football teams to push prams they would never have pushed before. It's nice that, as we sit chatting to the sound of our children's children laughing, they still know me by my maiden name. This is where I belong!

CHAPTER 15

Modern Dublin – When the Celtic Tiger Prowled

Dublin in the 1970s and early 1980s was quite a bleak city. Unemployment was very high, and the average industrial wage was quite low, at €2,500 per annum. The Northern Troubles were a constant backdrop to the times, with reports of shootings and bombings on an almost daily basis. Dublin had been bombed during World War II, when German bombs fell on Sandycove in 1940 and, the following year, on the South Circular Road and the North Strand, but the Northern Troubles eventually caught up with the capital city when in May 1974 three car bombs exploded in the city centre killing thirty-three people and injuring scores of others. Many of the buildings in the city centre had become derelict during this time and Dublin Corporation secured these by the insertion of unsightly steel props to avoid collapse.

Memorial to the victims of the 1974 bombings, Talbot Street.

Ireland's entry into the European Economic Community (later the EU) accelerated economic growth but two major oil crises, in 1973 and 1979, increased the cost of energy, leading to very high inflation which forced up the cost of living. This

Trinity College
Dublin, 1990.
*Reproduced courtesy of
the National Library of
Ireland.*

precipitated industrial unrest, causing regular strikes in the city and beyond.

Traffic congestion was heavy, resulting in regular smog and air pollution. In pre-Luas and DART days, Dubliners struggled to report for work on time and housing sprawled unchecked into the green hinterlands of the city as thousands of 'baby boomers', born after World War II, settled down.

Crime

In '70s and '80s Dublin criminal gangs invested in drugs, which caused huge damage among underprivileged communities. As the gangs grew in strength the city became a violent arena where drug barons marked their territory and fought among themselves with increasing levels of violence. Crime increased exponentially despite the best efforts of the gardaí.

Cornelius Gunning

Cornelius Gunning grew up in Ballyfermot and left school at the age of thirteen. He has written two novels and over forty plays, some of which have been performed in Dublin. One of these was made into a short film. In this short chapter from Con's crime novel *Vengeance is Mine*, Hughie Hutchinson (Hutch) has gone to jail for a crime he did not commit. He is especially angry at the judge who convicted him. Having served five years in Mountjoy Prison, he is finally released and looks forward to seeing his girlfriend again, but things do not go to plan.

From *Vengeance is Mine*

A feeling of euphoria enveloped Hutch as he walked towards the city centre. He realised that he had enough money to hail a cab to take him to Ranelagh, where he lived, but he was savouring every moment of his newly acquired freedom and he just walked along at a steady pace. He noticed a lot of new buildings which had not been there before he went to prison, but he had to admit that Dublin hadn't really changed – the atmosphere was still as electric as it always had been.

He strode along, swinging his bag as he walked, listening to the city noises, and feeling very much at home. He turned into a pub and sat for an hour; drank a couple of pints and listened to the conversations going on around him. He felt completely at ease with himself. Gradually, the nightmare of the past five years was overtaken by a dream of his future.

When he left the pub, he decided not to delay any further. Tonight would be a celebration for him, and for Danielle. Danielle, his girlfriend, was a very good-looking tall blonde lady. She was an only child and had had every advantage in life. She had done her degree in Trinity College. She worked as an administrative assistant for an international company. She travelled abroad, frequently, and often had to entertain visiting businessmen. However, she had no interest in them – they chatted her up in vain. Danielle wanted to get married and settle down. Her main ambition was to have a nice home of her own and two children.

It had taken his imprisonment to make Hutch realise how much she meant to him. She hadn't visited him in prison, but she knew he wouldn't have wanted her near the place. She had written to him after he first went to prison, but he didn't reply – she didn't expect any.

He bought a bottle of whiskey and a six-pack of beer and, knowing that his own phone was no longer connected, he rang Danielle from a pay phone.

A child answered the phone. Taken aback, he was silent for a moment and then he asked if he could speak to Danielle. In a few minutes her voice came down the line.

'Hi Danielle, it's me, Hutch. I'm back!' He almost shouted in his excitement. 'How are things? Did you miss me?'

Ranelagh.

'Hi Hutch, how are you?' Her voice sounded hesitant.

'Is everything okay, Danielle?'

'Yes, everything's fine.'

'I'm just on my way home now, but I couldn't wait to ring you. Can I meet you tonight?'

'Hutch, I'm sorry. I can't meet you. Obviously, you haven't heard. I'm married – have been for the past three and a half years. In fact, I have two children.'

'Geeze, Danielle, I never knew a thing.' Hutch was devastated, but he wasn't going to let it show in his voice.

'I wouldn't have rung you if I'd known. I hope he's good to you, and that you're happy. See you around, maybe. Goodbye.' He put the receiver down quickly, gave the side of the phone booth a despairing kick and ran to catch the bus he could see coming up the road.

He wasn't prepared to dwell on the feelings that were churning inside him, so he concentrated on getting to his house. When he got off the bus, he practically ran the last few metres to his house.

He stopped dead at the front gate and gasped for breath, as if he had been given a punch in the stomach. He couldn't believe it. The garden was completely overgrown and littered with empty bottles and other discarded rubbish; the gate was swinging on one hinge; the paint was peeling off the door and windows and, worst of all, one of the windows was smashed.

He pushed his way through the gate and rushed to the door. He opened it and stood aghast at the scene which confronted him. The place was like a tip-head. Obviously, someone had used his home as a squat in his absence. He staggered from room to room. He could feel the bile rising in his throat, and made his way, retching, to the bathroom.

'The bastards,' he muttered, 'the filthy bastards. I'll kill them when I find them!' There wasn't a single corner of the house that had escaped defilement.

He finally threw himself into a chair in the sitting room. He opened the bottle of whiskey, which he had intended to share with Danielle, to celebrate his release. Knowing there wasn't a clean glass or cup in the house, he just tipped back his head and gulped straight from the bottle.

He continued to enunciate the punishment he would mete out to the pigs who had so abused his home. But, as he drank, he gradually realised the futility of his thoughts. He could search for years and never find the rats responsible for this invasion and wreckage. His anger and rage transferred, by degrees, from those who were unknown to him to the 'One' who *was* known to him – the one responsible for his incarceration and, therefore, ultimately responsible for the carnage: Judge Broderick! Judge Broderick was the one who had caused him to be locked up; who had prevented his release weeks beforehand; who lost him his girlfriend to another man and also, logically, he was the one who enabled the vandals to enter his house to cause this destruction. He was the only one who would pay.

'Broderick, you bastard!' He yelled into the stale atmosphere that surrounded him. 'Broderick, you fucking bastard, beware! You will pay for what you have done to me. You will pay dearly. I'll make sure it hurts. Believe me, Broderick, if I have to die in the attempt, I'll make you pay!'

The whiskey bottle soon lay empty on the floor. Hutch lay sprawled in the chair and, through his drunkenness he screamed 'Vengeance is mine, Broderick, vengeance is mine, vengeance is mine!' – until he finally passed out where he lay.

While the Celtic Tiger Prowled

From the 1990s onward the Irish economy improved, with an excellent road network linking the capital city to all parts of Ireland – financed by the EU Regional Fund. The introduction of bus lanes combined with the rail services of DART and Luas (2004) went some way to cutting down on traffic congestion. The M50 carriageway, built between 1983 and 2010, further improved congestion, although it would, in time, become congested itself, especially during morning and evening rush hours.

A ban on bituminous coal helped improve air quality in the city hugely, reducing smog. Many new features improved the face of Dublin City, from the updated Guinness Storehouse (2000) to IMMA (Irish Museum of Modern Art) in Kilmainham. The Dublin Port Tunnel was opened in 2006, further freeing up space on Dublin's roads as heavy vehicles used this route instead.

'The Celtic Tiger' was a term used to describe the Irish economy from the late 1990s until the economic crash of 2008. The economy grew rapidly during these years, resulting in a 'property bubble', which eventually 'burst' and a serious recession ensued. During this

The Port Tunnel.

time, however, with a buoyant economy and jobs readily available, many emigrants decided to return to Ireland from England and the USA to start afresh.

The Returned HiCo

Economist, writer, journalist, broadcaster, commentator and documentary-maker David McWilliams has written five books. He is famous for such neologisms as 'HiCo Man' and 'Breakfast Roll Man'. The following extract from David's *The Pope's Children* describes the 'HiCo man' – a returned emigrant, a mixture of traditional Irish and modern cosmopolitan. This man is taking his children to a match in Croke Park between Meath and Dublin.

From *The Pope's Children*

On his way to the ground, HiCo man passes young lads drinking on the banks of the canal and on towards the legions of Dubs outside Quinns on the top of Clonliffe Road, poured into their Arnott's strips, kissing the three castles[1] for the RTÉ cameras. The atmosphere is electric and unthreatening. This is a family affair. There are as many little girls in Meath jerseys as lads in the blue of the city.

In the old days, before the spread of the Babybelt, Dubs and Culchies[2] knew who was who. But in recent years that has blurred. I noticed this recently playing a soccer match in Ratoath, Co. Meath. The accents of those on the Ratoath team perplexed me. Half the lads had the pure Meath *patois*, dropping the 'r's everywhere. The other half were unadulterated Cabra. I was in the Babybelt – home of the Kells Angels – where Dubs become Culchies and Culchies become Dubs. I was playing against the new breed, the first generation commuters, the Dulchies.

Dulchies and their kids were very much in evidence as they walked down to the Canal End. A father in neutral colours with a daughter in full Dubs rig-out was holding hands with her younger brother who was head to toe in the green and yellow of the Royal County. The family's

1 The three castles appear on the Dublin City coat of arms.

2 A pejorative term for a rural dweller, as distinct from a Jackeen or Dubliner.

The Pogues, *c.*1988.

divided loyalties reflect the bad planning, traffic, ten-hour crèches and multinationals that symbolise the Dulchies, or Royal Blues as they are called in Navan.

When HiCo man reaches the vertiginous upper echelons of the Canal End, the true feat of engineering becomes evident. The stadium is magnificent, but as impressive as the view and the pitch are the loos. There are loads of them and they are spotless. You see, the HiCo is a very practical dreamer which comes from reading all those design magazines. He learned the value of organisation, planning and bathroom sensibilities while in the US. He is part of the first generation of Irishmen who worries about the length of queues in women's loos. The GAA's concern about women's loos places them on a higher evolutionary plane than their soccer and rugby alickadoo[3] counterparts. However, despite being at the top of their game, the GAA still cannot prevent the new Irish speculation craze from infecting the Holy Grail. Companies that bought the corporate boxes for a song in the 1990s are now taking advantage of the huge upsurge in corporate entertainment in the full-on nation and are flogging them off to the highest bidder for the All-Ireland final. This is the sporting equivalent of the property auctions page.

Looking down at his two children, Eamonn and Niamh, he never really thought he would be here. For all those years in London and New York he had avoided the Tayto-crisps shillelagh-ism of Setanta Sports, Irish

3 A person associated with football or rugby who does not actually play the game.

bars and Kilburn High Road. There were of course some notable exceptions to this rule, Giant's stadium, any Pogues gig and 'The Crying Game' to name but a few. But his Irishness had been ambiguous. Like all his peers he left here more than he was pushed. He wanted a brownstone in New York, a roof-terrace in Primrose Hill, an apartment in the Marais. He wanted a lifestyle commensurate with his education. He got out to imbibe possibilities, to embrace cosmopolitanism and to achieve a career that Ireland could never offer. In fact, for most of the 1990s he was a self-loathing Irishman and the last thing he was going to do was create a home-from-home in London, New York or Paris. Like many of our 200,000 returned emigrants he is much better educated than those who stayed behind. ...

The HiCo migrant accredited to his invented Ireland everything that was the opposite of London or New York. Where the metropolitans were busy, Ireland was slow; where they were greedy, Ireland was generous; where New Yorkers were unfriendly, Dubliners were salt of the earth; where London was polluted, Ireland was clean, and so on. Ireland became for him and many others, an invented place which offered an idyllic lifestyle. It was jammed with wholesome things like communities, families and schools with dedicated teachers, houses with gardens and sagacious savants who knew how to put life before work. It was their escape valve from the obsessive compulsive behaviour of corporate America. ...

The game begins. The Dubs start badly and immediately are four points down. Gradually they claw themselves back. The stadium is an explosion of colour. The Hill is a sea of blue – flags, hats, fliers and San Siro-esque flares. The stands are green and yellow, banners are unfurled, and children hurl unspeakable abuse at the ref who is a dot on the horizon. The noise builds. Every challenge is replayed, recounted and reworked by the aficionados. The Dubs win in the end.

Out on the street, in the looming shade of the enormous stand, a huge Guinness poster symbolically obscures the entrance to Holy Cross College and the Archbishop's Palace. There was a time when the Bishop himself threw the ball in. No longer. The GAA has ditched the Bishop and brought back the pagans. The scene is dark and menacing, a muscular young Setanta faces a half dog/half wolf – the Cú of Cúchulainn. The skies blacken over. The scene is the Bog of Allen in winter. But we know the script; the youthful hero tosses the *sliotar*[4] high, draws back, muscles bulging, pulls, makes perfect full-on contact. The ash almost smashed on impact, the *sliotar* bullets through the air straight down the throat of the snarling hound, who keels over. The legend of Cúchulainn is born. 'Guinness, live the legend' states the ad. In the words of historian Roy Foster, there we go again, 'telling tales and making it up in Ireland'.

The returned emigrant heads for home, the legend still alive. He and his tribe have come home – these Hibernian Cosmopolitan nomads, the elite of the Pope's Children, with their own ideas of how things should be done and how the country should be run.

4 A hard leather ball, similar in size to a tennis ball, which is used in hurling.

Theo Dorgan

Theo Dorgan is a poet, novelist, editor, librettist, essayist, translator, non-fiction prose writer and documentary-maker, as well as an accomplished sailor. His work has been translated into many languages. In this poem about Croke Park, Theo captures the pre-match atmosphere but, on another level, uses the location to consider all those who have passed on over the years and to contemplate the transient nature of the lives of those who still survive.

Croke Park

We stand for the anthem, buoying and tribal, heart
    beating with heart,
our colours brave, our faces turned from the
    uncertain sun.
The man beside me takes my hand; good luck to
    yours, he says;

I squeeze his calloused palm and then – he's gone.

Croke Park.

A shadow socket where he was, the one beside him
    vanishes
and another before me, behind me; all around Croke
    Park
one by one we wink out of existence: tens, hundreds,
    then
thousands, the great arena emptying out, the wind
    curling in
from the open world to gather us all away. Each
    single one of us.
I could feel myself fail at the end, but then maybe
    everyone thought that,
each one of us the last to go. The whistle blew and
    we all
came back with a roar, everything brighter and louder,
    desperate and vivid.
I held his hand a moment longer, I wished his team
    all the luck in the world.

Marian Keyes

International bestselling author Marian Keyes has
sold over 35 million copies of her novels and has had
them translated into thirty-three languages. Born in
Limerick and raised in Cork, she has a degree in law
and now lives in Dún Laoghaire in Dublin.

In this excerpt from *The Woman Who Stole My Life*, Stella Sweeney is a Dublin mother of two teenage children, Betsy and Jeffrey, and is recovered from a debilitating disease which rendered her paralysed and incapable of speech. She has been restored to health by a dashing neurologist, Mannix Taylor. After his marriage fails, he contacts Stella and asks to meet her. Although Stella's own marriage to Ryan is over, her sister Karen, with whom she works in a beauty parlour, advises her against getting involved. Stella still agrees, however, to meet Mannix by the sea in Dún Laoghaire.

From *The Woman Who Stole My Life*

On Tuesday morning, I checked my appointments: I had nobody in at one o'clock.

'Is it okay if I go to lunch at one?' I asked Karen.

'Are you mad? That's our busiest time.'

'Grand,' I said mildly. We'd see.

While I was waiting for my ten o'clock appointment, I decided to give myself a pedicure. As I exfoliated my feet with vigour, Karen watched me with narrowed eyes. 'You're putting a lot of work into that. You make sure you charge yourself for it.'

'I'm equal owner of this salon, Karen. I know our system.'

'It's all going to go horribly wrong, you know.'

'What is?'

'Whatever is going on with you and Mannix Taylor.'

'Nothing's going on.'

'You've lost your mind. Splitting up with Ryan.'

'It's been over for a long time with Ryan.'

'Things were grand before Friday. Until you heard Mannix Taylor was single.'

'What colour should I do my toes?'

She clicked her tongue and left the room.

By one fifteen, no walk-ins had appeared, so I grabbed my coat and said to Karen, 'I'm going out.' Then I belted down the stairs before she could stop me, wondering if he'd still be there.

When I saw him sitting on the bench, staring out to sea, I felt like I'd had a blow to my chest. I was as breathless as if I was fourteen and this was my first ever date. It was dreadful.

At the sound of my footsteps, he looked up. Gratitude seemed to wash over him.

'You came,' he said.

'You waited,' I replied.

'I've already waited a long time for you,' he said, 'what's another half-hour?'

'Don't say things like that.' I perched on the edge of the bench. 'It's too ... slick.'

'I've brought sandwiches.' He indicated a brown paper bag. 'Let's play a game.'

Startled, we looked each other in the eye. We both swallowed hard.

I cleared my throat and asked, 'What's the game?'

'If I've managed to bring your favourite sandwich, you meet me again tomorrow.'

'I like cheese,' I said cautiously. I was afraid of him producing turkey and cranberry, my most hated.

'What kind of cheese?' he asked.

'... Any kind.'

'Go on. Be specific.'

'... Mozzarella.'

'I got you mozzarella and tomato.'

'That's my favourite,' I said, almost fearfully. 'How did you know?'

'Because I know you,' he said. 'I *know* you.'

Dún Laoghaire harbour.

'Jesus Christ,' I muttered, pressing my hand over my eyes. This was way too heavy.

'And,' he added, almost breezily, 'I bought eight sandwiches. One was bound to be something you like ... but just because I made sure I was right doesn't mean it wasn't meant to be. Either way, it means you've got to meet me again tomorrow.'

'Why? What do you want from me?' I felt on the edge of tears. Five days ago I'd been a long-term happily married woman.

'I want ...' He looked into my eyes. 'You. I want, you know ... The usual.'

'The usual!'

'I want to lie you down on a bed of rose petals. I want to cover you with kisses.'

That silenced me for a while. 'Is that from a song or something?'

'I think it might be Bon Jovi. But I'd still like to do it.'

'What if you're a weirdo who only likes me mute and paralysed?'

'We'll soon find out.'

'But what if I've started to like you?' It was already way too late for that. 'In all seriousness, do you do this sort of thing a lot?'

'What? Fall in love with my patients? No.'

'*Are* you a weirdo?'

After a pause, he said. 'I don't know if this counts, but I'm on antidepressants.'

'For what?'

'Gout.'

He laughed and I stared at him.

'Depression,' he said. 'Mild depression.'

'This isn't funny. What kind of depression? Manic?'

'Just the ordinary kind. The kind that everybody has.'

'I don't.'

'And maybe that's why I like you.'

'I have to go back to work.'

'Take a sandwich for your sister. I've got six spares. Go on.' He showed me the inside of the paper bag, which was rammed with sandwiches. I took a beef and horse-radish and put it in my bag along with my own uneaten one.

'See you tomorrow,' he said.

'You won't.'

Back at the salon, Karen greeted me sourly. 'How's Mannix Taylor?'

'He sent you a present.' I smirked into her baleful face and handed over the sandwich.

'I never eat carbs.'

'But if you did, beef and horseradish would be your favourite.'

'How did he know?' She was interested, despite herself.

'That's the kind of man he is,' I shrugged, like it was no big deal.

He wants to lie me down on a bed of rose petals and cover me with kisses, I told myself. In which case I'd want to get busy. I went at my bikini area with the laser, then did a full agonising half-hour of the anti-cellulite machine on my thighs, then – disregarding all safety regulations – immediately gave myself a full-body spray tan.

Wednesday was another dry, bright-blue day, very unusual weather for Ireland. Cold, though, bitterly cold. But I couldn't feel it even though I'd worn my not-warm, show-off coat that I only ever wore from car to restaurant, just long enough for everyone to say, 'God, your coat is gorgeous!'

Once again I was almost thirty minutes late, and yet there he was, sitting on the bench, staring out to sea, waiting for me.

'I have your sandwiches,' he said.

I accepted without enthusiasm. There was no point; I couldn't eat it. I'd barely been able to swallow a mouthful since Monday.

'Can I ask you things,' I said. 'Like where do you live now?'

'Stepaside. A rented flat. Georgie has the house. Until we sort out all the ... you know, legal stuff.'

'Where's the house?'

'Leeson Street.'

Stepaside, South
Dublin.

Almost in the city centre. Not in a rural retreat near the Druid's Glen, like I'd imagined. All that detail I'd put into the life I'd invented for him ...

'No one else talked to me in hospital,' I realised. 'You were the only one who treated me like an actual person.' ...

'And you were like my jailer, the good-cop one who shoves pieces of bread under the door.' My anger grew. 'I was vulnerable. And you took advantage of that. I want to go now.'

I was on my feet and he stood up too, anxiety all over his face.

'Tomorrow?' he asked.

'No. Definitely not. Maybe. I don't know.' I hurried away and immediately became entangled with a number of gangly, untucked[5] schoolboys who were clearly on the mitch.[6]

On Thursday morning, I said to Karen, 'I won't be going out today at all.'

'Good,' she said, with satisfaction.

'You can take the day off, I'll cover everything.'

'I'm not taking the day off, you eejit. Paul Rolles is booked in for a back, sack and crack wax at one o'clock.'

Brightly, I said, 'I'll do that.'

'He's my client,' Karen said. 'He's decent, tips big and he trusts me.'

5   Out on the loose.
6   Playing truant
    from school.

'Let me do him today. You can have the tip anyway.'

'Okay.'

At one o'clock I welcomed Paul in and got his clothes off and got him up on the bed and started whipping strips off his back, and as I thought of Mannix sitting on the pier waiting with my sandwich, I felt pleased with myself and my iron willpower.

I was chatting away with Paul, a cat lover, and I was doing the automatic-pilot thing that counts as beautician talk: 'Go on.' 'Did she?' 'Climbed the curtains all by herself?' 'God, that's gas.' 'She sounds like a right mad yoke!'[7]

But my head was elsewhere. This Paul was a big bloke and even though I was going at warp speed, waxing him was taking a long time. As I painted on the molten wax and pressed down the fabric strips, then whipped them off, I was like a wire that was stretching tighter and tighter. 'Stick your bum up, good man. I'll just get in between your –' Paint, press, whip. Paint, press, whip. PaintPressWhip. PaintPressWhip.

It was about ten to two when, coming at Paul's testicles from the rear, the wire inside me snapped. 'I'm really sorry, Paul, but I'm going to ask my sister to step in to finish you off.'

'What –' Paul sat up on his elbows, his bare bum in the air, looking very vulnerable.

'Karen?'

She was on her stool, at the desk.

'Karen.' My voice was high and wobbly, 'Would you mind stepping in and tidying up Paul? All done except the ... you know, last bit. I've suddenly remembered that I need to pop out.'

Her eyes blazed with rage, but she couldn't berate me in front of a customer.

'Of course,' she said, through lips that didn't move.

I was already pulling on my coat. I hurried down the stairs, trying to put on lipgloss as I ran. ...

When I arrived at our bench, Mannix said, 'Can you believe the weather?'

7 'Yoke' is Hiberno-English for any object or thing.

'We're talking about the weather?' I was almost contemptuous. But I looked up at the sky – it was still freakishly bright-blue and cloud-free, like God was conspiring to bring Mannix and me together.

'One day soon it'll rain,' Mannix said.

'And ...?'

The meaningful look in his eye made me scoot along the bench, away from him.

He too scooted along the bench and he grabbed my wrist.

'We'll have to meet in another place.'

'And ...?'

'Exactly,' he said. 'And ... think about it.'

I looked at my lap, then gave him a sideways glance. He meant the bed of rose petals and everything that went with it.

Then my attention snapped to something else entirely – I'd just seen someone I knew. It was so unlikely that I had to be imagining it. But I looked again and it was definitely him: Jeffrey.

Horrified, my gaze locked with his.

I stammered, 'You ... you should be at school.'

Jeffrey looked from Mannix Taylor to me and yelled, 'And you should be a proper mom. I'm telling on you!'

'I haven't done anything!'

Jeffrey ran off and, wild-eyed, I said to Mannix, 'I have to go.'

I chased after Jeffrey and he must have heard me because he stopped and whirled around.

'They saw you,' he shouted. 'The guys in my class.'

What guys? Then I remembered the gang of schoolboys I'd bumped into the other day, and I could have wept. They'd been in Jeffrey's class? How about that for awful luck?

With a sinking heart, I realised that my bad deeds would always be found out.

Shame washed over me. Shame and sorrow for Jeffrey.

'Sweetheart, I'm sorry, please –'

'Get away from me. You whore!'

Dublin Flamenco

There are several versions of the following Dublin street ballad, which, it is believed, dates back to the seventeenth century. In all versions the speaker observes a beautiful Spanish lady who is involved in such activities as washing her feet, catching a moth in a net, brushing her hair and so on.

The Spanish Lady

As I came down through Dublin City
At the hour of twelve at night
Who should I spy but a Spanish lady
Washing her feet by the candlelight
First she washed them, then she dried them
Over a fire of amber coals
In all me life I ne'er did see
A maid so sweet about the soul

Whack for the Too Rye, ooh, Rye addy
Whack for the Too Rye, ooh, Rye aye
Whack for the Too Rye, ooh, Rye addy
Whack for the Too Rye, ooh, Rye aye

As I came back through Dublin City
At the hour of half past eight
Who should I spy but the Spanish lady
Brushing her hair in the broad daylight
First she brushed it, then she tossed it
On her lap was a silver comb
In all me life I ne'er did see
A maid so fair since I did roam

Woman in a Grey Shawl by a follower of Spanish painter Goya (1746–1838). *Reproduced courtesy of the National Gallery of Ireland.*

Whack for the Too Rye, ooh, Rye addy
Whack for the Too Rye, ooh, Rye aye
Whack for the Too Rye, ooh, Rye addy
Whack for the Too Rye, ooh, Rye aye

As I came back by Dublin City
As the sun began to set

Who should I spy but a Spanish lady
Catching a moth in a golden net
First she saw me, then she fled me
Lifting her petticoats o'er her knee
In all me life I ne'er did see
A maid so fair as the Spanish lady

Whack for the Too Rye, ooh, Rye addy
Whack for the Too Rye, ooh, Rye aye
Whack for the Too Rye, ooh, Rye addy
Whack for the Too Rye, ooh, Rye aye

I've wandered north and I have wondered south
Through Stoneybatter and Patrick's Close
Up and around, by the Gloucester Diamond[8]
And back by Napper Tandy's house[9]
Auld age has laid her hands on me
Cold as a fire of ashy coals
But where is the lovely Spanish lady
So neat and so sweet about the soul?

Whack for the Too Rye, ooh, Rye addy
Whack for the Too Rye, ooh, Rye aye
Whack for the Too Rye, ooh, Rye addy
Whack for the Too Rye, ooh, Rye aye

8 A famous Dublin pub that lay at the diamond-shaped intersection of Sean McDermott Street and Gloucester Place.

9 James Napper Tandy (1740–1803) was an Irish revolutionary and member of the United Irishmen. Since Tandy lived in ten separate houses in Dublin it is hard to be specific here.

Ross O'Carroll Kelly

Paul Howard is an author and journalist as well as being a prolific award-winning comic writer. He is the creator of the fictional character Ross O'Carroll Kelly, a rugby jock who lives in the affluent south suburbs of Dublin and who speaks with the middle-class accent that has been described as 'Dortspeak' (from the area through which the DART train passes). Howard satirises the nouveau riche in his comic novels and points up their inflated social aspirations. He recreates the accent of such people: *orm* for *arm*, *goys* for *guys*, *hordens* for *hardens* and so on, as well as the confusing expression 'yeah, no'.

The DART line, Dalkey.

In the following excerpt from *Operation Trumpsformation*, Ross O'Carroll Kelly has cheated on his wife, Sorcha, and has been thrown out of his house. He comes back to visit unexpectedly, where he finds another man there feeding his triplet children, but all is not what it seems.

From *Operation Trumpsformation*

I don't believe it. And I mean that quite literally. The code for the gate has been changed, I put in 2, 0, 0, 9 – the first year that Leinster won the Heineken Cup – but nothing happens. Then I try 2, 0, 1, 1 – the second year that Leinster won the Heineken Cup – except it ends up not being that *either*? So then I try 2, 0, 1, 2 – God we won a lot of Heineken Cups – and that's when I hear Sorcha's voice coming through the intercom.

She's like, 'What do you want, Ross?' and she sounds more *sad* than angry?

I look up at the security camera and I go, 'Yeah, no, you changed the code.'

She's there, 'I asked you what you wanted, Ross?'

'Er,' I go, 'obviously I want to get in.'

She's like, 'Ross, what part of "Our marriage is over!" do you not understand?'

Ross O'Carroll-Kelly,
Eason, O'Connell
Street.

10 A famous retired
    Irish rugby player.

11 The Happy Pear
    are twins Stephen
    and David Flynn,
    authors and
    restauranteurs who
    promote healthy,
    plant-based food.

12 A pun on
    'Jedward', the
    combined names
    of twins John
    and Edward
    Grimes who sing
    and present TV
    programmes.

'I don't accept that it is over. I'm hoping you can find it in your heart to forgive me for what I did.'

I rode a woman in Dalkey.

She goes, 'We agreed that Saturday was your day to see the children. You can't just turn up randomly like this.'

And I'm there, 'I'm not turning up randomly. I, er, forgot something. When you focked me out.'

'What did you forget?'

'Yeah, no, my Rugby Tactics Book.'

'Your Rugby Tactics Book? Okay, do you actually need it?'

'Is that a serious question?'

'As in, do you need it right now? Could it not wait until the weekend?'

'After my heroics for Seapoint last week, I have to accept that a lot of clubs are going to be sniffing around me now – maybe not as a player, but there's a coaching role out there for me. That book contains my whole, I don't know, psychology on the game.'

The gate suddenly pops open, and in I go. I trudge up the gravel driveway towards the gaff. She's standing on the doorstep with her orms folded tightly. I'm a good reader of body language. She definitely still wants me.

I'm there, 'You look well.'

She doesn't. She looks like shit – like she hasn't slept for the past week. I suppose it's possible that she hasn't.

She goes, 'Just take whatever you came for, then go, Ross,' refusing even to look at me. ...

I tip downstairs with the book under my orm. Sorcha is still standing by the front door – again with her orms folded. I'm like, 'So how have you been?'

She goes, 'How the fock do you think I've been, Ross?'

Sorcha *never* swears? Except when she's with her closest female friends and they're all talking dirty, usually about Gordon D'Arcy[10] or one of the Happy Pear[11] goys. Vegward,[12] as I call them.

I'm there, 'I know I'm repeating myself here, but that woman meant nothing. She put it on a plate for me. Made it nearly impossible for me to say no.'

She burst into tears. She goes, 'You focking ruined everything, you stupid focking ... focker! And for what, Ross? For what?'

'It doesn't have to be the end, Sorcha.'

'Do you honestly think I can just pretend it never happened?'

'Hey, you've done it before – why not?'

She dries her eyes with the tips of her fingers, then her expression suddenly *hordens*? 'Not this time,' she goes. 'I deserve better.'

I don't think she means that. I notice she's still wearing her wedding and engagement rings. That's hopefully a sign she might still take me back.

I'm there, 'Can I see the kids?'

She goes, 'You can see them Saturday – like we agreed.'

'Saturday is days away.'

She lets out a roar at me then. She goes, 'You should have thought of that before you slept with that focking slut!'

I'm there, 'Okay, sorry,' and I'm just about to walk out the door when events suddenly take what might be described as a turn.

I hear a voice – a *dude's* voice? – coming from the kitchen. It's like, 'Are you going to eat your breakfasht, Leo?' ...

I'm like, 'Who the fock is that?'

Sorcha goes, 'It's none of your business who it is, Ross.'

And I'm there, 'None of my business? I've only moved out, what, a week? And already some random dude is giving my children their breakfast.'

'He's not some random dude. His name *happens* to be Magnus.'

'Magnus?' ...

I head for the kitchen in an absolute rage, with Sorcha following me, going, 'Ross, no! Get out! Get out of this house now!'

I push the kitchen door. Honor is sitting at the table. Brian, Johnny and Leo are in their high chairs. Their faces obviously light up when they see me, but I'm more interested in the total stranger who's trying to get them to eat their unsweetened quinoa porridge with mashed Bortlett pear. What makes it even worse is that the dude – yeah, no I'm going to admit this – is a seriously good-looking goy. He's like, blond, square jaw and six-foot-three, possibly six-foot-four in height – which I wouldn't have thought was Sorcha's type. She was always more into backs than forwards.

I somehow resist the temptation to straightaway deck him. Instead I just go, 'Who the fock are you?'

'Oh my God,' Honor goes, obviously delighted by all this development. 'Plot twist!'

'Hey, I'm Magnush,' the dude has the balls to go on, 'and you mush be Rosh. Shorcha's hushband, yesh?'

I'm picking up an accent – it sounds like Drogheda or somewhere up that way.

'Maybe I should have been more specific,' I go. 'Who the fock are you and what the fock are you doing in my house?' ...

This Magnus dude goes, 'Well at thish moment I am giving the cheeldren their breakfasht. Shorcha, you should eat shome breakfasht, too. I'm shorry to tell you that your wife and I heff been up all night.'

That ends up being the line that snaps my crayons. I literally launch myself across the kitchen at the dude. I don't give a fock how tall he is. I grab him by the front of his shirt and I slam him up against the two-door American fridge-freezer.

Sorcha actually screams. She's like, 'Nooo!!!' ...

He's tugging at my fingers trying to loosen the grip I have on him. 'What ish ... what ish wrong?' he manages to go.

'You and my wife,' I go, 'up all night, were you? And you say it to me in front of my kids?'

Sorcha storts grabbing me, going, 'Ross, it's not what you think!' ...

I cock my fist, ready to drive it into the dude's big handsome face when all of a sudden I feel something crack me across the back of the skull, causing me to release my grip and hit the deck. When my head clears, which takes a good thirty seconds, I notice that it's the Le Creuset cast-iron square Grillit that I bought Sorcha last year.

Cast-iron square Grillit.

'Get out!' she goes, screaming at me at the top of her voice. 'Get out of this house!'

I'm there, 'Seriously, Sorcha?' climbing to my feet and checking the back of my head for blood. 'I haven't been gone a week and you've already moved on. But you were the one who mentioned "slut" earlier.' ...

Sorcha's like, 'I haven't moved on!' still roaring at me, by the way. 'This is Magnus, our new manny!'

Oh, shit.

I'm there, 'Your manny? What the fock is a manny?'

She's like, 'What does it sound like, Ross? He's a male nanny. I said I was going to hire someone to help me with the children while I'm working on the campaign.'

'What campaign?'

'Oh my God, I told you weeks ago that me and Muirgheal are going to be working for the Yes side in the same-sex marriage campaign.'

She's there, 'I told you that once we'd tackled the whole Africa thing, marriage equality was next.'

'Yeah,' I go, 'the whole BGT thing. See, I *was* listening?'

'BGT is *Britain's Got Talent*. The *actual* acronym is LGBT. But then I wouldn't expect you to know that.'

'I thought you were hiring, like, a nanny. I'm not sure I like the idea of another man living under my roof.' ...

Magnus is like, 'Well you heff nothing to worry about from me on that shcore – right, Shorcha? Becaush I am gay.'

I'm like, 'Gay? Hang on, what did you mean when you said the two of you were up all night?'

'I'm shorry,' he goes, 'shometimes my English ish – how to shay? – not sho good.'

'Where are you even from? I would have put money on Louth. You talk like one of the Kearneys.'

'I'm from Finland.'

'Finland?'

Yeah, no, it's a new one on me as well.

I'm there, 'Random.'

'Not that it's any of your business,' Sorcha goes, 'but he was helping me write a speech. I'm giving a talk this morning to my grandmother's Active Retirement group. We're trying to win over the horts and minds of senior voters who have a more conservative view of marriage.'

Paula Meehan

Award-winning Dubliner Paula Meehan, professor of poetry, poet, dramatist and children's author, has had her poems set to music and seen them translated into many languages. She has conducted residencies in universities and prisons.

The following poem describes a woman making her way home through the Dublin streets, keenly attuned to the sights and sounds around her, yet anxious about her personal safety until she has turned the key in her door. The poem is part of a sequence of urban poems entitled 'City'.

Birdy by Rowan Gillespie, Mount Street Crescent.

Night Walk

Out here you can breathe.
Between showers, the street
empty. Forget your lover
faithless in the chilly bed
who'll wake soon and wonder
if you've left for good.
Granite under your feet
Glitters, nearby a siren, Threat

or a promise? You take Fumbally Lane
to the Blackpitts, cut by the canal.
Hardly a sound you've made, creature

of night in grey jeans and desert
    boots,
familiar of shade. Listen.
                  The train
bearing chemicals to Mayo, a dog far
    off, the fall
of petals to the paths of the Square,
a child screaming in a third floor flat.

On Mount Street high heels clack,
stumble in their rhythm, resume.[13]
Let her too get home safe, your
    prayer,
not like that poor woman last night
dragged down Glovers Alley, raped
    there,
battered to a pulp. Still unnamed.
Your key in the door, you've made it back,
a chorus of birds predicting light.

St Stephen's Church
(the 'pepper cannister')
on Mount Street.

13 Many Dublin sex
   workers are seen
   by night on Mount
   Street.

CHAPTER 16

New Dubliners

Since the days of the Celtic Tiger immigrants have been arriving in Dublin from a variety of countries – Nigeria, Sierre Leone, Sudan, Poland, Hungary, Romania, the Czech Republic, China, India, Pakistan, the Philippines and many more. Apart from those in the professions, a large percentage of immigrants can be seen in the catering business, where one hears a variety of accents in hotels and restaurants, while others work in Dublin hospitals as nurses and ward attendants or as taxi drivers. The father of Finglas-born former Gaelic footballer Jason Sherlock – who played between 1995 and 2010 and distinguished himself on the Dublin team – was originally from Hong Kong and his mother is Irish. In 2017 3,200 candidates were granted Irish citizenship at a ceremony in the Convention Centre, Dublin. This ceremony is now held outside Dublin in such towns as Limerick and Killarney.

Taxi rank, St Stephen's Green.

Laura Gerulyté Griffin

Laura Gerulyté Griffin comes from the Baltic port of Klaipéda in Lithuania, but she has lived in Ireland

Dublin Airport.

for many years and written journalistic articles. Her blog on LinkedIn is entitled 'Think Outside the Fox'. The following article was written for *The Journal*. Here Laura describes her experience of the city, its people and its turns of phrase.

An Immigrant's Experience of Dublin

I knew very little about Ireland when I moved to Dublin over fourteen years ago. I could have described the country in three things: Guinness, U2 and the IRA.

My first impression of Dublin was as a tiny grey city, full of dark pubs, surrounded by endless bleak suburbs. And the rain rarely stopped.

However, Dublin wasn't just a dirty old town. Over time I discovered that the city had a lot to offer – beautiful beaches, spectacular Dublin hills and the majestic Phoenix Park. I wanted to make it work, to make Dublin and Ireland my home.

I arrived with very little English, relying on friends to get me settled. After a while I realised I wasn't living in Ireland, more like a small unofficial enclave of Lithuania and so I knew that to properly integrate I'd need to leave my comfort zone.

I left a house I shared with fifteen other Lithuanians and moved in with two Irish strangers. I didn't get lectures on Yeats, Lavery or Wilde but I learned that chocolate tastes better if it's chilled in the fridge. I was taught how to make crisp sandwiches as hangover treats.

Salt and vinegar flavour was a revelation to me even though my first attempt was like swallowing acid-coated razor blades. I even picked Lyons tea over Barry's and religiously drank a milky cup of tea at least five times a day.

I purchased *Donnie Darko* and put it on the shelf in my bedroom, joining the ranks of Irish people who owned a copy. However, at the end of my first year, I still felt lonely and isolated in my Swords apartment, but my English was getting better each day and that gave me strength.

As the years passed, I learned that making friends with Irish people wasn't as easy as I thought it would be.

They were all good craic and full of promises to meet up again but most rarely bothered. In a way I understood them, they had their circle of friends, why should they bother with someone new. I was told that the Irish were the friendliest bunch in the world and yet I couldn't make connections.

Fáilte Sord 2018, Swords.

I tried harder. I listened to Marian Finucane and I rarely missed *Prime Time*. By then I knew that Pat Kenny was much better on the radio than on TV.

After three years I was adding a 'sh' sound at the end of words and putting a heavy emphasis on my 'u' sounds.

I tried to lose the hard Eastern European rolling Rrrr and sound more like posh D4-types and salt of the earth Dubliners at the same time. 'Rightsh, butsh, D-UH-nnes Stores, always bettsher value, D-UH-blin b-UH-s.'

The result was a ridiculous mish-mash of an accent. My social network was still made up of five or six fellow foreigners and my original Lithuanian ex-pats.

Over fourteen years later I finally have a solid circle of friends. What happened? The answer is I don't really know. Maybe Irish people need to feel that you are not going anywhere. Maybe I was just lucky enough to meet the right people at the right time. I guess I will never completely know why but I do hope that other people have an easier time.

Ireland may be the land of a thousand welcomes but there's a difference between friendly and friendship. You still need to stick your foot in the door to keep it open long enough so that people will eventually let you inside.

Anna Cooper

Anna Cooper is a graduate of Adam Mickiewicz University in Poznań, Poland, with a master's in Polish philology and a master's in library and information studies from UCD. She is currently living in Ireland and is librarian in the Alton Library of St Vincent's, Castleknock College. Here she describes her early experiences as an immigrant.

An Immigrant's Perspective

Sometimes I think that leaving your native country is the hardest test you may need to endure in your entire life. But, on the other hand, it is also one of the most fascinating adventures ...

I still remember the overwhelming excitement and fear that gripped me when I saw that enormous Ryanair plane we were about to board. Back then people from my country did not really fly that often. I was the first member of my whole family to travel by plane. In order to get from Poland to Ireland you had to travel to the UK first and then spend eight daunting hours at London Stansted Airport for a transfer to Dublin and the unknown.

We came to Ireland in October 2005, bursting with excitement and apprehension but with limited funds in our pockets. I travelled with my best friend, newly graduated from university and a little disappointed with the poor prospects that the Polish job market had to offer us. We were so scared! But we were also desperate; ready to work very hard and prepared to challenge and

overcome our own personal weaknesses, especially the language barrier.

Grafton Street.

A mutual friend, who moved to Ireland one month before us, collected us from the airport and organised our first accommodation: a single bedroom in a terraced building in Dublin. We shared the house with three Irishmen, and this was where the fun began.

Our biggest concern was that our English would not be proficient enough to communicate effectively, and that people would laugh at us or get fed up waiting for our well-thought, but slowly-constructed responses. Of course, we never experienced any of that. On the contrary, Irish people were always very patient and understanding regarding our communication skills. We were so utterly overwhelmed by the support we received from the Irish; from the instructions on how to get your PPS number sorted, from our housemates, the politeness of public sector clerks and patience of bus drivers, we felt really welcome.

Our initial experiences of integrating into the Irish way of life were positive and quite often hilarious. At the beginning we were thought to be Russian. It was a great opportunity to exercise our patriotism and national pride and we spent long moments explaining that, 'We are Polish, you know, Solidarity and Lech Wałęsa and then

The Temple Bar pub, Temple Bar.

the fall of the Berlin Wall.' We were usually met with the excited response of 'Oh yes, great stuff!'

Then came the language: the confusion when you were asked 'what's the story?' or, better still, 'what's the craic?' We were both working for a big manufacturing company, with multinational and multiregional personnel, and it was the best English immersion course we could dream of. Soon we were able to distinguish between various Irish accents, and shortly after, we were able, successfully, to greet the Siobhans and Diarmuids! We learned how to pronounce properly words with 'h' and 'u'. Overall, it was a truly fascinating experience.

The longer we lived in Ireland, the more we travelled. Dublin came first and appeared to us a city of so many interlinking contrasts: with its monumental neoclassical buildings, converging glass and steel structures, with the GPO facing the Spire, and the enormous lush green Phoenix Park in the middle. From smiling gardaí, who would happily give you directions to your bus stop, flower ladies, shouting out their special offers, to street performers on Grafton Street and in Temple Bar, we were charmed! But first and foremost, at its very core, this city was multinational. The sense of openness and acceptance was overwhelming. It was like being in a melting pot, and that sense could well describe the whole island. The novel combined with the traditional resulted in a warm and vibrant degree of curiosity.

We were enchanted by the landscape of Ireland – mysterious round towers, old graveyards, twisted stone bridges and the gems of Glendalough, Ben Bulben, Valencia Island, Connemara National Park, Killarney, Cliffs of Moher and Croagh Patrick, to name but a few. Sometimes it felt like you were in an ancient poem or in a realm from Tolkien's world.

The Irish mentality adds to the charm of the island. They are not afraid of the new and the different while constantly expanding and developing. We always admired the way Irish people attempted to preserve and promote their native language and folk culture. Their positive attitude married their stoic pride, but without undue pomposity. It was a unique experience to observe Irish people singing their national anthem with all their hearts, as last orders were called in the pub having already enjoyed one too many Guinnesses! We were never treated like strangers here. The hospitality and the positive attitude of the Irish made us feel at home.

Many things have changed since I first stepped out of that big, scary Ryanair plane. I've changed jobs and requalified. Literature was always my passion and I loved teaching. I wanted to work with young people, and, after completing my postgraduate degree at UCD, I worked first in public, and then in school libraries. I find myself very fortunate. On a daily basis, I manage a kingdom of curiosity and knowledge, and I am able to aid young people on their journey to self-awareness and fulfilment.

Our school library is a welcoming and nurturing place. Students come here to read, to do some research and to work on their homework. Enjoyment, however, should be at the very heart of this safe place, so it makes me happy to know that they also visit the library to have some fun. Every month, we have three vibrant reading and discussion clubs (always with chocolate biscuits)! I receive great support from my teaching colleagues, and we run many projects together. This year we have already had themed reading festivals, a heated Spelling Bee competition, well-being and poetry workshops, interactive subject projects, and Scrabble tournaments as well as a welcoming visit from a well-known author. The school's management recognises the importance of literacy promotion, and we try to fulfil all reading needs and cater both for reluctant readers and advanced Manga fans. It's like a birthday celebration every week; my favourite moment being when a student or staff member comes and is not sure what to read, and then we browse the shelves together. Could you ask for more? I do what I love every day. My motto for my job is the popular Chinese proverb: 'Choose a job you love, and you will never have to work a day in your life.' I could not agree with this more.

With new challenges, career opportunities and personal satisfaction comes a new perspective. I feel so immersed here now; I rarely describe myself as an immigrant! My family life revolves largely around Irish traditions and rituals that I now pride myself in calling my own. My child is bilingual, and she can recite poems in Irish, we have our turkey for Christmas and even celebrate 'The Boys in Green' rugby achievements.

Irish openness and tolerance stole my heart. A famous Polish poet, Władysław Broniewski, once said that '[social] existence determines consciousness'. Although his poem was praising common effort in building a socialist people's republic, I couldn't agree more with the idea that 'your home is where you feel you belong, where you are needed and where you can flourish'. For me it's here, among green fields with stone walls and winding narrow roads.

Eileen Casey

Here Offaly-born, award-winning poet Eileen Casey, while travelling on the Luas, sees an African man running to catch the tram. As he runs nimbly, she imagines him as a graceful Masai warrior. This is an interesting portrait of an immigrant in Dublin, especially when contrasted with the poet's recollection of a fair day in the Midlands. Eileen now lives in Tallaght, Dublin. She is the editor of *The Lea-Green Down: New Poems by Established and Emerging Poets Inspired by the Poetry of Patrick Kavanagh*.

Warriors

The Grand Canal is silvery as a new coin.
I'm on the Luas thinking of nothing in particular
when a man, swift as an antelope,
runs from the houses towards Suir road.

Legs, long as spears, gather speed.
This Luas is a wild one

The Grand Canal.

broken free from the herd.

On the grass, thawing frost steams a mirage,
dust rises.
His winter coat, shirt and navy trousers
dissolve to gorgeous Masai colours.
He gleams like the skin on these tracks,
each muscle and sinew
zig zagging a perfect quarter arc

bearing down on the metal beast,
and I'm back on the Midland streets

side-stepping pools of greenish-
hued cow dung. Straw
straggles from trailers, haggling
wasps swarm around my ears.

A cow breaks from a loose bunch
is chased by a farmer in breeches
held up with braces, his face berry red,
legs akimbo; the stick in his hand
orchestrating a fair day.

Later, there'll be whiskey in the pubs,
chocolate for children of the tribe
creeping in to sit on the long benches.

My warrior comes on board
scarcely out of breath. Beyond

Rialto
Fatima
St. James's
Heuston Station

we journey towards the city.

Mihaela Dragan

Mihaela Dragan was born in Bucharest, Romania. Having taught for ten years, she graduated from the University of Bucharest with a degree in history and philosophy. She then went on to study law. Since her childhood, she has dreamed of becoming a writer. Mihaela is a poet who writes in Romanian and English. She has lived in Dublin and, since she has read the best of Irish writing in her youth, is very familiar with literary Dublin as the following article demonstrates. Her Romanian novel *Love in a Cup of Coffee* was published in 2020.

Dublin: A Cultural Perspective

Most of the time, the city boasts a cheerful atmosphere, experienced around the Spire, which seems to support a huge white cloud, transforming this modern steel monument, built by Ian Ritchie Architects, into a cotton candy.

When wet and chipped, as often happens, the Spire becomes a giant invisible umbrella handle, trying in vain to protect us from rain.

Sometimes, the Spire pokes through the air in a cold and threatening manner, reminding me of the stakes of the bloody Voivode Vlad the Impaler, who used to impale

Trinity College.

Turkish prisoners, thus becoming – over the centuries – the source of inspiration for Bram Stoker's famous novel *Dracula*. Count Dracula is presented by Dr Van Helsing as 'that Voivode Dracula who won his name against the Turk, over the great river on the very frontier of Turkey-land'.

As a metaphorical return to the principles of geometry, despised by the inhabitants of the famous Laputa from *Gulliver's Travels*, whose applications they considered to be 'vulgar and mechanical' (Jonathan Swift), the steel cone is a manifestation of modernity, perhaps as controversial as the Berkeley Library of Trinity College Dublin, which astonished everyone fifty years ago with its brutalist architectural style. Both steel and reinforced concrete, seem a far cry from the redbrick shade of the Georgian architecture. They emerged on the map of Dublin, like an exclamation mark and square brackets [...] carrying the mirage of modernity from the old European continent.

In October 2017, Paul Kolarek (a young architect in 1967, when he was selected to build the new library) met with young students and steered the conversation between generations into a sensational step back into the past, perhaps because Dublin is the perfect setting for open, curious and friendly dialogue. For an East European like me, this brutalist style is not at all unfamiliar; the niches, configured in specific reading spaces between the reinforced concrete walls, preserve architectural symbolism of the continent, reminding me, in particular, of one of the founders of the avant-garde DADA movement – Marcel Iancu, a famous architect born in Romania, who later moved to Israel, whose modern buildings in interwar Bucharest anticipated the new urban transformation that emerged in the wake of World War II.

The library still retains furniture from 1967, with simple lines, clear colours; still carrying ergonomic prints created over fifty years ago, which enhance the tranquillity necessary for reading and studying in more modern times. Light floods the space generously, covering the book pages, apart from the miraculous touch of the magic lamp beams in the reading room of the old Library of Trinity College Dublin.

In front of the Berkeley Library, the masterpiece of the famous Italian sculptor Arnaldo Pomodoro 'Sphere Within Sphere', and sister sculpture of the 'Cortile della Pigna' masterpiece of the Vatican Museum (Rome), focuses and reflects images breaking the perfect and magical form of the sphere, a symbol used by alchemists in the past. It is the embodiment of Pomodoro's artistic manifesto, which states that 'the sphere is a marvellous object, from the world of magic and wizards, whether it is of crystal or bronze, or full of water ...'

As for the internal layers, 'these look like the gears or cogwheels of a complex machine, symbolizing the fragility and complexity of the world.'

As my thoughts drift inside the bronze innards of the sphere, my mind delights in the symbolism of Constantin Brâncuși, whose artworks displayed at MOMA influenced Pomodoro in 1959 to such an extent that immediately after seeing the sculptor's masterpieces he entered a phase of 'monumental outdoor sculptures, enhancing and changing shapes', confessing: 'I felt their force with deep emotion, but at the same time I experienced a wish to destroy their perfections.'

And just as in Jonathan Swift's description in *Gulliver's Travels* of a dinner of geometric dimensions served in Laputa – 'For the first course, there was a shoulder of mutton cut into an equilateral triangle, a piece of beef into rhomboids, and a pudding into a cycloid' – I hunger for the symbols of this city, unable to quench my desire to discover and smell it, sipping and chewing it in large gulps.

This bustling Viking city, with its old medieval manuscripts, of which the Book of Kells remains a gem, has gradually made way for new narratives, some real, some historical, and others downright fabulous, moving from its insular isolation to the sensibility of the Old Continent to earn well-deserved Nobel prizes for literature.

On the cobblestones, Ulysses's steps transform the city into a Roman set, as the imaginary route chimes in real time to our footsteps. Our task is simply to choose the direction and to understand the present meaning.

James Joyce by Marjorie Fitzgibbon, North Earl Street.

If you walk past James Joyce's statue, towards O'Connell Street Lower, then turn right on O'Connell Street Upper, and right again onto Cathedral Street, you will end up at St Mary's Pro Cathedral, where every Sunday the enchanting voices of the Palestrina Choir waft from inside. This boys' choir was founded in 1890 by Dr Vincent O'Brien and established with the invaluable help of Edward Martyn, who is well known as one of the co-founders of the Abbey Theatre, along with W.B. Yeats, Lady Gregory and George Moore. The old Latin liturgical music transports one back to other times. ...

Going further towards Henry Street and then walking for about 200 metres, continuing on to Mary Street about 300 metres more, within fourteen minutes of Arran Quay, you will come to the junction where the Bar Council–Law Library lies beside St Michan's Church.

Of course, you will chance upon, not just black legal robes, but the world of Bram Stoker's classic, inspired by the gothic atmosphere of mummies preserved in the vaults of the church. Here lawyers go about their business past that church in whose crypts lie undiscovered mysteries. Actually, *Dracula* begins with the journey of the unassuming London lawyer, Jonathan Harker, whose journey in the novel marries reality and fantasy.

Time stands still at St Michan's, the yard covered in lush green vegetation among ancient tombstones dating back to 1095 when the church was founded – the same year that Pope Urban II publicly announced the First Crusade at his synod, for the liberation of the Holy Land from the Muslims. Bearing witness to this time is, reputedly, the mummy of a 6 feet 5 inch man, returned from bloody Byzantium, whose warlike and mystical ambience is captured by W.B. Yeats in his poem, 'Sailing to Byzantium'.

Inside the church one finds the organ on which, in 1742, George Frideric Handel played the 'Messiah' for the first time, an oratorio which soon became one of the most beloved choral works in western music and which delighted Jonathan Swift, dean of St Patrick's Cathedral, whose boys' choir joined the Dublin premiere, just three years before his death. ...

I believe each Dublin sunset contains the dreamy aspirations of young girls, as John Keats described them in 'The Eve of St Agnes', that romantic poem from the Middle Ages, rewritten in forty-two Spenserian stanzas. Not content to remain in verse, they are reborn in Harry Clarke's stained glasses, more sensual, more erotic, and more fascinating, as the light filters through his stained glass at the Hugh Lane Gallery to bring us the story and inspire our dreams. The silhouettes of Clarke's characters, the strong colours in bold shades of fuchsia and electric blue, the bold lines of the soft and sensual arms bring together, in a unique way, the medieval world with the sharp rhythm of action in Keats's poem. And like a never-ending story, Harry Clarke has other unusual window-

sized stained glass, at the famous Bewley's coffee house on Grafton Street, which occupies a special place in the hearts of Dubliners. ...

Bewley's Café, Grafton Street, showing four decorative windows by Harry Clarke (1928).

All we have to do is enter Bewley's, and pass through the vanilla-coloured panels, at the entrance to the café, bringing the musk and fragrance of cypress from the Far East, to understand Clarke's stained-glass invitation to visit the gardens.

One recalls Field Marshal Arthur Wellesley, 1st Duke of Wellington, one of the famous students of Whyte's Academy on Grafton Street, which inhabits the spot where you just drank coffee – Bewley's Oriental Café. Walk towards the Phoenix Park, leave behind the Ha'penny pedestrian bridge, originally called the Wellington Bridge, erected just a year after the Duke's famous victory at Waterloo. In the euphoria following his victory, the Phoenix Park Memorial was erected – considered to be the largest stone obelisk in Europe. If Dublin citizens voted against this obelisk being erected in Merrion Square, the Iron Duke (pseudonym for the Duke of Wellington) now has his revenge with the Spire piercing the heart of the city! From the height of the obelisk one looks down on the Phoenix Park and the River Liffey, the construction combining the course of history with the beauty of art.

Royal Hospital
Kilmainham gardens.

On Wellington's coat of arms, we note the Latin inscription *Virtutis Fortuna Comes* ('Fortune is the Companion of Virtue') as we cross the river to the Formal Gardens of the Royal Hospital Kilmainham – an iconic building that dates from the late seventeenth century. Greek statues and geometric topiary adorn these beautiful spaces. Here is housed the Irish Museum of Modern Art. Baroque architecture and stained-glass windows, in perfect harmony with the seventeenth-century landscape, give way to contemporary art, of which the most original is the Freud Project (2016–21).

If you look at the military walls of the Royal Hospital Kilmainham, guarding the inner court of IMMA, from the stairs to the main gallery, through the red filters of plastic glass sheets, all will be absorbed into a rosy, translucent view of the perfectly aligned window walls and the colour game will become a wonderful kaleidoscopic exercise, which children will enjoy so much. Beyond lies Kilmainham Gaol, an old prison dating from 1796, in which the leaders of the 1916 rebellion were imprisoned and executed.

White gulls fly over the trees, like light handkerchiefs, puzzled perhaps how other birds can be frozen in bronze forever in the Garden of Remembrance. Here the figures of the Children of Lir – Oisín Kelly's famous sculpture – represent the struggle for Irish freedom, achieved after centuries, in 1922.

A year later W.B. Yeats was awarded the Nobel Prize in Literature, returning to a new, more confident nation, still scarred by the Civil War. This optimism is shared by Dubliners today, who still celebrate the past – although willing to embrace new cultural experiences.

Maybe this is why I have never felt like a stranger here in Dublin, no matter where I roam. Perhaps it's because I had already experienced the best of Irish literature before I came to live here. Little did I dream, as a child who wanted, like Gulliver, to travel to Lilliput, that I would later visit St Patrick's Cathedral, where Jonathan Swift himself was dean, or that I would get to read poems at the Irish Writers Centre, overlooking the Garden of Remembrance.

CHAPTER 17

Last Melodies

Finglas writer Dermot Bolger has achieved international fame as a poet, novelist, short story writer and dramatist. In 2022 he was awarded an honorary doctorate in literature from the National University of Ireland.

In this powerful poem, Dermot poignantly recalls his mother taking him, as a child, to the hospital for speech therapy. Despite his speech difficulties, Dermot went on to distinguish himself nationally and internationally as a prolific writer.

Temple Street Children's University Hospital.

Temple Street Children's Hospital
This is your territory, I brought you here:
Shoddy tenement windows where washing
    flaps,
Crumbling lanes where cars get broken for
    parts.

There is an archway beneath which we
    passed –
Like the one above which you shared a flat
With your sisters up from Monaghan for work

In a war-becalmed Dublin. Surely you must
    once

Have gazed up, puzzled by how the years since
Had landed you here with a son, a stuttering misfit,

Unable to pronounce the most simple of words;
A bright penny whose cloud you'd never see lift
As you fretted, unaware of how close death hovered.

The speech therapist's office had fancy toys and
    books
And a special mirror which allowed me to be
    watched.
The waiting room contained a white merciless clock

That ticked off the final hours we spent alone,
Gazing down at a garden where I yearned to walk;
Trapped indoors by the shame of my garbled tongue.

*

I stand outside that hospital in Nerney's Court,
At Kelly's Row where a blacksmith once worked,

And no logic can explain why you feel this close,
Why I see us in the mother and child who pass,

Or how, as I age, I slowly become your son,
Gazing through your eyes with incomprehension.

I was too young to have known you, so it makes no
    sense
That every passing year only deepens your absence.

Strong Dublin Men

The provenance of this Dublin street ballad is uncertain
but the reference to the Jeffries–Johnson fight in 1910 –
which saw the black American reigning champion Jack
Johnson knock out his white challenger James Jeffries
after fifteen rounds – places the song in the 1920s.

    The chorus, which allows audience participation,
has made the ballad very popular.

The Big Strong Man (Sylvest)

Have you heard about the big strong man?
He lived in a caravan.
Have you heard about the Jeffries–
Johnson fight?
Oh, what hell of a fight!
Well you can take all the
heavyweights you've got
I know a lad who'd beat the whole
lot.
He used to ring the bell in the belfry
and tonight he's gonna fight Jack
Dempsey.

James Jeffries and Jack
Johnson.

Chorus

He was my brother Sylvest (what's
he got?)
A row of forty medals on his chest (big chest!)
He killed fifty badmen in the west
He knows no rest, big is the man, hellfire
Don't push, just shove, plenty of room for you and
me!
He's got an arm (got an arm!)
Like a leg (like a leg!) a lady's leg!
And a punch that could sink a battle ship (big ship!)
It takes all the army and the navy to put the wind up
Sylvest.

Well he'd thought he'd take a trip to Italy
And he thought he'd like to go by sea.
He jumped off the harbour in New York
And he swam like a man made of Cork (Corkman!)
Well he saw the *Lusitania* in distress (what'd he do?)
He put the *Lusitania* on his chest (big chest!)
He drank all the water in the sea and he walked all
the way to Italy.

Chorus

Well he thought he'd take a trip to old Japan
And he thought he'd bring the whole brass band.
He played every instrument they got
And like a lad he played the whole damn lot.
Well the old church bells did ring (ding dong)
And the church choirs did sing (la la!)
They all came out to scream and shout for my big
brother Sylvest.

Chorus

Leaving the City
Attributed to the Galway poet D.K. Gavan, the
lyrics to the following song were added to an original
Irish slip jig. The ballad describes the adventures and
mishaps of a young man from Tuam in County Galway
as he leaves home, first for Dublin City and then on to
Liverpool. Perhaps the best interpretation of the song
is by the late Luke Kelly and the Dubliners.

The Rocky Road to Dublin
While in the merry month of May, now from me
    home I started
Left the girls of Tuam nearly broken-hearted
Saluted father dear, kissed me darling mother
Drank a pint of beer, me grief and tears to smother
Then off to reap the corn, and leave where I was born
Cut a stout blackthorn to banish ghosts and goblins
A brand-new pair of brogues to rattle over the bogs
And frighten all the dogs on the rocky road to Dublin

Chorus
A-one, two, three, four, five
Hunt the hare and turn her down the rocky road
And all the ways to Dublin, whack, follol de-dah

In Mullingar that night I rested limbs so weary
Started by daylight next morning, blithe and early
Took a drop of pure to keep me heart from shrinking

That's the Paddy's cure when'er he's
    on for drinking
To hear the lassies smile, laughing all
    the while
At me curious style, 'twould set your
    heart a-bubblin'
They asked me was I hired and wages
    I required
Till I was almost tired of the rocky road
    to Dublin

Chorus

In Dublin next arrived, I thought it
    such a pity
To be so soon deprived a view of that
    fine city
So then I took a stroll, all among the
    quality
Bundle it was stolen, in a neat locality
Something crossed me mind, when I looked behind
No bundle could I find upon me stick a-wobblin'
'Quiring after the rogue, said me Connaught brogue
It wasn't much in vogue on the rocky road to Dublin

The Ha'penny Bridge
from the Merchant's
Arch.

Chorus

From there I got away, me spirits never falling
Landed on the quay, just as the ship was sailing
Captain at me roared, said that no room had he
When I jumped aboard, a cabin found for Paddy
Down among the pigs, did some hearty rigs
I played some hearty jigs, the water round me
    bubbling
When off Holyhead I wished meself was dead
Or better far instead on the rocky road to Dublin

Chorus

The boys of Liverpool, when we safely landed
Called meself a fool, I could no longer stand it
Blood began to boil, temper I was losing
Poor old Erin's Isle they began abusing
'Hurrah me soul' says I, me shillelagh I let fly
Galway boys were by and saw I was a hobblin'
With a 'lo!' and 'hurray!' they joined in the affray
Quickly cleared the way for the rocky road to Dublin

Chorus

Permissions

We offer our sincere thanks to the following for permission to use the poems, excerpts and prose pieces in this book. 'On Raglan Road' and 'Canal Bank Walk' by Patrick Kavanagh are reprinted from *Collected Poems*, edited by Antoinette Quinn (Allen Lane, 2004), by kind permission of the Trustees of the Estate of the late Katherine B. Kavanagh, through the Jonathan Williams Literary Agency. 'Temple Street Children's Hospital' from *That Which is Suddenly Precious* by Dermot Bolger, published by New Island Books, is reprinted by permission of the author. Thanks to Gill Books for 'HiCo Man', excerpted from *The Pope's Children* by David McWilliams; Mercier Press for the chapter from *Beyond the Breakwater* by Catherine Foley; New Island Books for 'First Night at the Abbey' from *The Splendid Years* by Máire Nic Shiúbhlaigh with Edward Kenny, edited by David Kenny; Eileen Casey for 'Warriors'; Marie Gahan for 'From Galtymore to Greenhills'; Catherine Ann Cullen for 'Spike City'; Poolbeg Press for 'Boozing with the Borstal Boy', excerpted from *Me Darlin' Dublin's Dead and Gone* by Bill Kelly; Carcanet Press Ltd for 'The Huguenot Graveyard at the Heart of the City' by Eavan Boland; Dedalus Press for 'Croke Park' by Theo Dorgan, 'Liffey Swim' from *Liffey Swim* by

Jessica Traynor, 'Night Walk' from *Mysteries of Home* by Paula Meehan, and 'A School' from *The Sundays of Eternity* by Gerard Smyth; Cork University Press for the excerpt from *Luke Kelly: A Memoir* by Des Geraghty; Penguin Random House for excerpts from *The Woman Who Stole My Life* by Marian Keyes, *Operation Trumpsformation* by Paul Howard, *A Star Called Henry* by Roddy Doyle, and *Borstal Boy* by Brendan Behan; James Lawless for 'Ascending a Liberties Stairway in 1952', from *Rus in Urbe*, originally published by Doghouse; Richard Barnwall for 'Memories of the Old North Road'; Anna Cooper for 'An Immigrant's Perspective'; Mihaela Dragan for 'Dublin: A Cultural Perspective'; Clothesline Press for 'Philo' by Pauline Fayne and 'The Globe on Captains Road' by Teri Murray; Laura Gerulyté Griffin for 'An Immigrant's Experience of Dublin'; Cló Iar Chonnacht for 'Faoileán Drochmhúinte' and 'Mo Thaibhse' by Mairtín Ó Direáin; Mark Jenkins for 'The Liberties of Dublin'; Con Gunning for the excerpt from *Vengeance is Mine*.

Image Credits

Acknowledgements: p. 13, The National Library of Wales/Wikimedia; Introduction: p. 18, The Print Collector/Alamy Stock Photo/W6P6X9; p. 19, Stephen Reid/Internet Archive Book Images/Flickr; Chapter 1: p. 26, littleny/iStock/458310187; p. 27, Noel Bennett/iStock/1284766892; p. 28, National Gallery of Ireland/NGI.899; p. 37, illustration from *The Missing Ship* by W.H.G. Kingston, London: Griffith, 1890; Chapter 2: p. 39, Mnavi/Wikimedia; Hohum/Wikimedia; p. 40, Joe King/Wikimedia; p. 43, Michael Fitzgerald/Xn4/Wikimedia; p. 45, Damien Slattery/Wikimedia; p. 48, Leslie Noelle Sullivan/Wikimedia; p. 49, Alexis Jazz/Wikimedia; Chapter 3: p. 55, MrPenguin21/Wikimedia; p. 56, ManfredHugh/Wikimedia; p. 57, Mu/Wikimedia; p. 58, David M. Jensen/Wikimedia; p. 60, Adam Cuerden/Wikimedia;

p. 62, C.W. Eckersberg/Rsteen/Wikimedia; p. 63, Napoleon Sarony/Library of Congress/Wikimedia; p. 64, Cygnis insignis/Wikimedia; Chapter 4: p. 69, Adolf Hoffmeister/NoJin/Wikimedia; p. 72, Noel Bennett/iStock/1169010561; p. 73, Noel Bennett/iStock/1171904083; p. 75, William Murphy/Flickr; p. 80, CartesPostalesDub/Wikimedia; p. 82, Sarah777/Wikimedia; p. 90, National Library of Ireland/EAS_1682; p. 95, National Library of Ireland/L_ROY_00679; p. 96, National Library of Ireland/L_ROY_03114; Chapter 5: p. 100, National Library of Ireland/INDR 2995; Chapter 6: p. 106, National Library of Ireland/WIL 34[7]; p. 108, Radharc Images/Alamy Stock Photo/RXPG2R; p. 110, XCalPab/Wikimedia; Chapter 7: p. 114, William Murphy/Wikimedia; p. 115, Jan Arkesteijn/Wikimedia; p. 117, psyberartist/Wikimedia; p. 118, James McDonald/Seamusmac/Wikimedia; p. 121, OsmanPhotos.com/Alamy Stock Photo/DW60B7; p. 123, National Library of Ireland/IND6.776; p. 127, National Library of Ireland/NPA ROBS136; p. 129, Piolinfax/Wikimedia; Chapter 8: p. 132, National Library of Ireland/ET C488; p. 134, National Library of Ireland/EPH E76; p. 136, Archidub1/Flickr; p. 138, Metro-Goldwyn-Mayer/Jack Jackie Pomi/Wikimedia; Chapter 9: p. 143, National Library of Ireland/KE 203; p. 144, Piaras Béaslaí Papers, 1895–1965/Graeme Bartlett/Wikimedia; p. 145, Rannpháirtí anaithnid/Wikimedia; p. 146, National Library of Ireland/KE 121; p. 149, John Singer Sargent/Wikimedia; p. 150, Walter Paget/One Night In Hackney/Wikimedia; p. 153, National Library of Ireland/NPA DOCG68; Chapter 10: p. 156, *The Complete Poems of Francis Ledwidge* (1919)/Londonjackbooks/Wikimedia; p. 157, National Library of Ireland/Eas 1909; p. 165, National Library of Ireland/NPA PERS77; p. 167, Sheila1988/Wikimedia; p. 168, Eweht/Wikimedia; Chapter 11: p. 169, George Petrie Esq. RHA/British Library/Flickr; Chapter 12: p. 175, Reginald Gray/Wikimedia; p. 178, Keystone Press/

Alamy Stock Photo/E0W0C4; p. 182, Jean Housen/ Wikimedia; p. 186, William Murphy/Wikimedia; Chapter 13: p. 188, Radharc Images/Alamy Stock Photo/GKK2K4; p. 190, OSU Special Collections and Archives: Commons/Flickr Commons; p. 192, William Murphy/Flickr; p. 197, William Murphy/ Flickr; Chapter 14: p. 203, National Library of Ireland/ TIL853; p. 204, World Image Archive/Alamy Stock Photo/2E8XPK3; p. 209, UtDicitur/Wikimedia; p. 210, PA Images/Alamy Stock Photo/G6DY7K; p. 212, Andrea and Stefan/Flickr; p. 215, Fisher, H. Son and Co., George Petrie, R. Winkles/Wikimedia; p. 218, Vinyls/Alamy Stock Photo/2H3NT44; p. 220, Rickybon/Wikimedia; Chapter 15: p. 228, National Library of Ireland/LPP_22/15; p. 230, William Murphy/Flickr; p. 232, Sarah777/Wikimedia; p. 234, Pictorial Press Ltd/Alamy Stock Photo/CB7F91; p. 237, Sheila1988/Wikipedia; p. 239, William Murphy/ Flickr; p. 245, National Gallery of Ireland/NGI.784; p. 247, Fergal/Wikimedia; p. 248, Stormy clouds/ Wikimedia; p. 252, Robert Linsdell/Wikimedia; p. 253, EliziR/Wikimedia; Chapter 16: p. 257, Rossyxan/ Wikimedia; p. 267, Toniher/Wikimedia; p. 269, Peter Cavanagh/Alamy Stock Photo/T4TR0X; Chapter 17: p. 275, Onceinawhile/Wikimedia.

Every effort has been made to contact the copyright holders of material reproduced. If any infringement of copyright has occurred, the owners of such copyright are requested to contact the publishers.

Bibliography

Bateson, Ray, *Dead and Buried in Dublin*, Meath: Irish Graves Publication, 2002.

Behan, Brendan, *Borstal Boy*, London: Arrow Books, 1990.

Boland, Eavan, *A Poet's Dublin*, Manchester: Carcanet Press, 2014.

Bolger, Dermot, *That Which is Suddenly Precious: New and Selected Poems*, Dublin: New Island Books, 2015.

Boran, Pat and Gerard Smyth (eds), *If Ever You Go: A Map of Dublin in Poetry and Song*, Dublin: Dedalus Press, 2014.

Casey, Eileen, *Drinking the Colour Blue*, Dublin: New Island Books, 2009.

Collinge, Declan, *Common Ground*, Dublin: Inisfail Press, 1996.

_____ *Fearful Symmetry*, Dublin: Mentor Books, 1990.

_____ *The Lonely Hush of Eve: Selected and New Poems*, Dublin: Mentor Books, 2014.

_____ *Súnámaí*, Dublin: Coiscéim, 2013.

Dolan, Terence Patrick, *A Dictionary of Hiberno-English*, Dublin: Gill and Macmillan, 1998.

Dorgan, Theo, 'Croke Park' from Pat Boran and Gerard Smyth (eds), *If Ever You Go: A Map of Dublin in Poetry and Song*, Dublin: Dedalus Press, 2014.

Doyle, Roddy, *A Star Called Henry*, London: Jonathan Cape, 1999.

English, Michael, *The Ha'penny Bridge*, Dublin: Dublin City Council, Four Courts Press, 2016.

Fayne, Pauline and Teri Murray, *A Childhood Unshared*, Dublin: Clothesline, 2011.

Foley, Catherine, *Beyond the Breakwater*, Cork: Mercier Press, 2018.

Gahan, Marie, 'From Galtymore to Greenhills' from Dermot Bolger (ed.), *County Lines: A Portrait of Life in South County Dublin*, Dublin: New Island Books, 2006.

Geraghty, Des, *Luke Kelly: A Memoir*, Cork: Cork University Press, 1994.

Gerulyté Griffin, Laura, 'An Immigrant Fits In', thejournal.ie, 14 April 2018.

Gunning, Cornelius, *Vengeance is Mine*, Dublin: Gunning, 2000.

Head, Richard, '17th Century Dublin' from Frank O'Connor (ed.), *A Book of Ireland*, London and Glasgow: Collins, 1959.

Hopkins, Frank, *Hidden Dublin*, Cork: Mercier Press, 2007.

Howard, Paul, *Operation Trumpsformation*, Dublin: Penguin Ireland, 2017.

Joyce, James, *A Portrait of the Artist as a Young Man* [1916], London: Granada Publishing, 1977.

_____ *Dubliners* [1914], London: Grafton Books, 1977.

_____ *Ulysses* [1922], London: Penguin Modern Classics, 2000.

_____ *Finnegans Wake* [1939], London: Penguin Modern Classics, 2000.

_____ 'Ecce Puer' [1932], poets.org.

Joyce, Patrick Weston, *English As We Speak It in Ireland*, Dublin: Wolfhound Press, 1979.

Kavanagh, Patrick, *Collected Poems*, Dublin: Penguin Random House, 2005.

Kelly, Bill, *Me Darlin' Dublin's Dead and Gone*, Dublin: Poolbeg Press, 1987.

Keyes, Marian, *The Woman Who Stole My Life*, Dublin: Penguin Books, 2014.

Kilfeather, Siobhán, *Dublin: A Cultural and Literary History*, Dublin: The Liffey Press, 2015.

Lawless, James, *Rus in Urbe*, Kerry: Doghouse, 2012.

Ledwidge, Francis, *The Complete Poems of Francis Ledwidge with Introduction by Lord Dunsany*, London: Hebert Jenkins, 1919.

Le Fanu, Joseph Sheridan, *The House by the Churchyard* [1863], gutenberg.org, 2006.

Liddy, Patrick, *Walking Dublin*, London: New Holland, 2004.

MacDonagh, Donagh, *Oxford Book of Irish Verse*, Oxford: Clarendon Press, 1958.

Mangan, James Clarence, 'My Dark Rosaleen', poetryfoundation.org.

McWilliams, David, *The Pope's Children*, Dublin: Gill and Macmillan, 2005.

Meehan, Paula, 'Night Walk' from *Mysteries of Home*, Dublin: Dedalus Press, 2013.

Murray, Teri and Pauline Fayne, *A Childhood Unshared*, Dublin: Clothesline, 2015.

Nic Shiúbhlaigh, Máire, with Edward Kenny, David Kenny (ed.), *The Splendid Years*, Dublin: New Island Books, 2016.

O'Connor, Frank, *A Book of Ireland*, London and Glasgow: Collins, 1959.

Ó Direáin, Mairtín, *Dánta: 1939–79*, Dublin: An Clóchomhar Tta, 1980; Indreabhán, Conamara: Cló Iar-Chonnacht, 2010.

O'Meara, Liam, *Francis Ledwidge: Poet, Activist and Soldier*, Dublin: Riposte Books, 2006.

———— *Zozimus: Life and Works of Michael Moran*, Dublin: Riposte Books, 2011.

Shelley, Percy Bysshe, 'On Robert Emmet's Grave', internetpoem.com.

Smyth, Gerard, *The Sundays of Eternity*, Dublin: Dedalus Press, 2020.

Stoker, Bram, *Dracula* [1897], London: Penguin Popular Classics, 1994.

Story Map, storymap.ie.

Swift, Jonathan, *The Works of the Rev. Jonathan Swift, Volume 9: An Examination of Certain Abuses in the City of Dublin* [1732], en.wikisource.org.

'The Dolocher', *Dublin Penny Journal*, Dublin, 1832.

Traynor, Jessica, *Liffey Swim*, Dublin: Dedalus Press, 2014.

Tynan, Katharine, *Collected Poems*, London: Macmillan, 1930.

Wilde, Oscar, 'The Selfish Giant' [1888] from *The Complete Illustrated Works of Oscar Wilde*, London: Bounty Books, 2004.

Yeats, W.B., *Michael Robartes and the Dancer*, London: Macmillan, 1921.